Praise for *Trust*

"A startling beginning kickstarts this straightforward memoir, and Flanagan immediately dives into her process of healing, serving as a guide while she gives readers a chance to experience her story and learn to heal their own wounds at the same time. Mixing Flanagan's story with her sincere advice is a refreshing approach. It's evident she speaks from experience, and her style offers readers the chance to personalize her wisdom for their own lives. Flanagan is honest and transparent, and her story is a good example of what it takes for someone to work through loss and addiction."

—BookLife Prize

"There is no one-size-fits-all way to navigate grief and addiction; the expansive self-help guide *Trust Yourself to Be All In* acknowledges this alongside an inspiring account of how one woman pieced together wisdom from a variety of philosophies to address her own trauma. Incorporating wisdom from Buddhism, Christianity, the social sciences, and New Age philosophies, this is a diverse but comprehensive guide to healing from loss. It espouses beliefs in souls and past lives and shifts blame for one's hardships to the individual soul, suggesting the importance of taking personal responsibility for actions and their outcomes."

—*Foreword* Clarion Reviews

"The loss of her beloved brother to a drug overdose sets a woman on a deeper quest for spiritual and emotional health in this memoir and self-help guide...Flanagan takes readers along on a tour of healing modalities, interspersing accounts of life events among descriptions of personal philosophy and deepening spirituality…she effectively stresses the value of working with therapists, writing in journals, and pursuing meditation throughout the book, and she goes into specific detail while doing so."

—*Kirkus Reviews*

"By sharing her lifetime of trauma and a "spiritual tapestry fabricated from the finest fibers of various belief systems," including Eastern religion, New Age spirituality, and the principles of Alcoholics Anonymous, Flanagan encourages readers to face their pain and develop unconditional self-love…a courageous act of full disclosure, a soul-cleansing the author encourages her readers to replicate in their own way to build trust in themselves and others, noting: "When you heal, I heal, and when we heal, the world heals."…anyone suffering from emotional angst, feelings of inferiority, or substance abuse will find kind, authentic guidance here to a life of greater peace, love, and forgiveness."

—*BlueInk Review*

"Turning the trauma and isolation of Covid into a triumphant period of self-growth and healing, Amanda McKoy Flanagan imbues each page of *Trust Yourself to Be All In* with uplifting energy and a clear hope for the world. Drawing largely from her personal experiences of pain, grief, self-sabotage, addiction, and eventual transcendence, this is both a raw memoir and a gentle guide…Both joyful and radical in its approach, *Trust Yourself to Be All In* is an uplifting and transformative read for people who have fallen into despair or are teetering on the edge. Focusing instead on compassion, love, trust, connection, and community, this polished and powerful book is recommended for readers looking for innovative ways to lift themselves out of modern malaise, which is so endemic to the current moment."

—*Self-Publishing Review*

Flanagan...lays bare her life story of how she finally found the path toward recovery and healing after almost 40 years of pain and grief while battling alcoholism, repressed childhood sexual trauma, dysfunctional relationships, and more...a true story of a woman's journey to get her life back on track, overcoming overwhelming odds along the way through sheer resilience and a dogged determination to live life to its fullest...a deeply personal story that will appeal to anyone who has suffered through loss and grief. Highly recommended."

—*Readers' Favorite*, 5-star review

"*Trust Yourself to Be All In: Safe to Love and Let Go* is a remarkable and intimate debut from Amanda McKoy Flanagan. To say this book spoke to me would tell only half the story; it also listened. Flanagan's intentional structuring of chapters and personal revelations creates a storytelling framework that leads the reader on a parallel journey to arrive at their own destinations and personal conclusions...a conversational, almost prescient narrative...a book written not to give answers, but to encourage the asking of questions, the perpetual seeking of truth."

—Joanna Monahan, author of *Something Better*

"Our world is suffering from collective pain. In *Trust Yourself to Be All In*, Amanda McKoy Flanagan shows us how this pain can inspire action, and from that action, we can truly heal. In this unflinchingly honest look into all our emotions and what it means to be human, Flanagan gives us every tool we need to live a life of meaning, despite the pain…An emotional masterclass on grief and healing. The book everyone needs right now."

—Rea Frey, award-winning, bestselling author of
Not Her Daughter and CEO of Writeway

"Trust Yourself to Be All In is an invaluable account of recognizing our self-destructive behaviors, being willing to change, and the importance of learning to love ourselves in order to love and be loved. No matter the cause of a person's emotional trauma, readers will relate to the self-deprecating depths of despair the author enters and be inspired by her vulnerable and brave accounts of healing."

—Christy Texeira, award-winning author of *Pink Elephants, A Mother's Story of Faith, Strength, and Perseverance*

"*Trust Yourself to Be All In* is a haunting memoir about love, loss, and recovery. Amanda's memoir is a riveting account of another Nietzschean insight: whatever doesn't kill me makes me stronger. She takes us on a journey through harrowing grief to self-forgiveness and healing. I was especially impressed with her discussion of Kintsugi, the Japanese art form that finds beauty in brokenness. Amanda is The Real McKoy."

—Jeffrey Berman, Distinguished Teaching
Professor of English, and author of *Dying to Teach:
A Memoir of Love, Loss, and Learning*

trust yourself
to be
all in

SAFE TO
LOVE
AND
LET GO

amanda mckoy flanagan

Trust Yourself to Be All In: Safe to Love and Let Go
Published by For Real Press
Castle Rock, CO

The events depicted in this book are authentic and all people are real. It is my story and to the best of my knowledge the events shared in this book are as they occurred. This book is not intended as a substitute for the medical advice of physicians or psychologists. The reader should consult a professional in matters relating to his/her health and particularly with respect to any symptoms that may require diagnosis or medical attention. Some material may elicit an intense emotional response.

Publisher's Cataloging-in-Publication data

Names: Flanagan, Amanda McKoy, author.
Title: Trust yourself to be all in : safe to love and let go / Amanda McKoy Flanagan.
Description: Includes bibliographical references. | Castle Rock, CO: For Real Press, 2023.
Identifiers: ISBN: 979-8-9856735-0-0 Subjects: LCSH Flanagan, Amanda McKoy. | Self-actualization (Psychology) | Self-esteem. | Self-reliance. | Conduct of life. | Spirituality. | Self help. | BISAC BIOGRAPHY & AUTOBIOGRAPHY / Personal Memoirs | BODY, MIND & SPIRIT / Inspiration & Personal Growth Classification: LCC BF637.S4 .F53 2023 | DDC 158.1/092--dc23
Cover and interior design by Victoria Wolf, wolfdesignandmarketing.com, copyright owned by Amanda McKoy Flanagan

QUANTITY PURCHASES: Schools, companies, professional groups, clubs, and other organizations may qualify for special terms when ordering quantities of this title. For information, email amanda@amandamckoyflanagan.com.

FOR REAL
PRESS

In honor of Jeremy S. McKoy
1/4/77 - 3/19/18 and beyond

For the grievers—of all the things, in all the ways.

"You and I are the force for transformation in the world. We are the consciousness that will define the nature of the reality we are moving into."

—Ram Dass, Love Serve
Remember Foundation

CONTENTS

WELCOME

I've descended into my shadow multiple times during my four decades on Earth. With each plunge, I've unearthed and exhumed the roots of my evil and my goodness. Every emergence gifted me with more enlightenment, emotional maturity, and gentle acceptance of my reality than I had before. If those times were plunges, then my self-imposed, year-long seclusion during the COVID-19 pandemic was like a four-hundred-foot nosedive into the bowels of my existence, into the deep. When I breached the surface, I gained an expanded view of what makes me tick and how that ticking is in tandem with the ticking of the collective. I became acutely aware of the denial of personal pain which, when healed, has the power to heal the world.

Three hundred sixty-five-plus days spent mostly at home gives a gal a lot of time to read, think, meditate, and learn. I had been afforded space to excavate and appraise roles, identities, values, and beliefs, both assigned to me and that I assigned to myself. On a nondescript day during my seclusion, I suddenly crossed the line I had been marking since beginning to work on the issues that kept me in a constant state of self-destruction, since the day I reclaimed my life as a sober woman. On this random day during the height of the pandemic, I crossed to the side marked "liberation." It was the end of the world I had been living in and the start of a brand new one. I was done allowing fear to control me and became willing to face my pain like never before.

Assembling the events that caused deep grief, creating a beautiful mosaic of the human I am meant to be, I carefully considered each situation and how it changed me, for good and for bad. I prayed for God to help me be gentle with myself and journaled extensively about where I had been and where I wound up, and it began to make sense. Finally. I then graced myself with the freedom to appreciate my achievements, weep for my losses, and open my arms to welcome what's next.

Once I allowed myself to get radically honest, I stepped boldly over the line. The side I crossed into housed a belief in myself and my worthiness, and the side I left behind was the dungeon where my chronic self-criticism, doubt, and shame resided. I traversed to the area stamped "nonnegotiable self-love" and could not turn back. Casting off the cape of beliefs that no longer served me—the cape of emotional self-protection—I made a decision to honor my soul's truth and became ready to take action on what matters to me with courage and authenticity.

My seclusion was my fast track to healing almost forty years of pain. It was the convergence of a decade and a half of spiritual research and application, of practicing tools required to initiate uncomfortable situations and exercise stamina to remain in uneasy feelings. It was the culmination of copious amounts of self-worth work. The result was unconditional love for myself and loving others to the best of my ability, on any given day, in any given circumstance.

Loss is a state we frequently find ourselves in and one we often resist feeling. Resistance leads to more pain as we believe we are not capable of loving others wholeheartedly and letting go of them peacefully. This distrust holds us back from being all in with others, producing painful disconnection. Once loss is dealt with, it has great potential to bring emotional security within, the needed element to create indivisible connection to ourselves and everything around us.

Regeneration of the pained spirit into feelings of safety, trust, and ultimately connection is possible when you acknowledge your grief warrants healing work, whatever your definition of grief may be. For some, acknowledging and communicating painful emotions is a highly dangerous activity, one that many avoid. Expressing pain is discouraged in society; we are insidiously urged to suppress the slightest sign of internal commotion upon its appearance. Somebody's crying; make it stop. Anxiety crops up; find a distraction. Detachment from thoughts, feelings, and emotions breeds disconnection from ourselves, leaving us insecure and unsafe in our skin. When we disconnect from ourselves, we disconnect from each other. This division, I believe, is at the heart of our pain.

We cannot detach from the internal commotion forever. It's impossible to dodge the elephant in the room indefinitely. The gigantic mammal in your face that you can see but don't want to feel will catch up with you eventually. This elephant, which is more like a woolly mammoth due to its monumental size and historic nature, will keep moving in on you no matter how hard you try to pen it back into its cage. So let's look at it. Let's talk about it.

Let's go all in and get real.

Pain is hard to grapple with. It is hard to step into. It's heavy and unpleasant but serves a purpose—a mighty one. Exploring feelings of life's pitfalls can usher in unconditional self-love, organically leading to a deep trust in yourself—both in a Higher Power and purpose and in others.

Self-love is *the* key to trust. It is the missing piece to complete the puzzle named joyous humanity. Before we can feel this overwhelming affection for self, we must connect with self. Self-connection often starts by acknowledging pain induced by a variety of losses, insecurities, and feelings of inadequacy, or a lack of belonging, among other grievances. Next, we find the courage to embrace the pain. Then, we acquire the strength to move through it and heal. Once healed, we connect with honesty, compassion, trust, and purpose—first to self, then to others.

Humanity is at a precipice, and connection is vital for continuing human evolution. Personally, connection is required for a fulfilling experience within our own hearts and minds; collectively, it is needed for sustaining the peaceful coexistence between mankind and nature. Love, the unifying driver of connection, must be steadily expressed to gain the momentum needed for healthy symbiotic relationships among all living things on Earth. It is the foundation upon which the building blocks of a harmonious society and planet rest.

We all have the potential and the duty to reach this state of love and connection, and it begins by trusting ourselves and each other to work together to make the changes demanded in this period of new consciousness: the New Earth. In this enlightenment period, authenticity and morality will trump societal pressure; the need for power and prestige (driven mostly by fear) will diminish.

I am not so idealistic (well, maybe a little) to suggest that doing this work will solve humanity's most profound challenges. However, the intention alone can bring a greater sense of safety, security, and community than we currently feel. We are ready and equipped with what we need to achieve this ideal. A plethora of written word, documentary films, and other information is available to guide us in the merging of the preternatural spirit (love) with the physical human (material). Let's bring the two into cohesion. It is our true nature, and when we act in accordance with our true nature like we are summoned to, we take the steps necessary to level up. Enlightenment and healing harmony is the end product—first felt within, then emerging and expounding outward. Harmony expounded returns as harmony within, and the cycle continues. The world and its people feel this healing energy, consciously and unconsciously, and we all benefit.

When you heal, I heal, and when we heal, the world heals.

The global community is suffering tremendously, and we are facing serious consequences from running from ourselves and each other. We must jump down into the emotional pit of pain that leads to disconnection to rise up in healing, love, and unity. Healing our pain will not only mend our tattered spirits but will repair the soul of the world. We have the power to do this. Together, we have more synergistic, powerful energy than ever. It's here, waiting for us to petition it. The time is now.

Will you take the leap? Will you allow yourself to feel the pain and the peace alive in the world around you? Are you ready to grow toward emotional evolution and spiritual ascension?

I hope so, because you are needed.

Although I find community at an Episcopal church, I do not endorse one spiritual school of thought or philosophy. Rather, I take a little from here and a little from there and knit a spiritual tapestry fabricated from the finest fibers of various belief systems, providing a beautiful design for living. If it resonates with my soul, I weave it into the confines of my psyche and my spirit.

This tapestry holds discoveries born from desperation and loss and from choices made that naturally separated me from the herd, leaving me disparate and afraid. Painful experiences told me I was worthless—a sorry excuse for a human, a troubled soul with little hope of a bright future, or any future at all. At least that's the story I told myself. That narrative got me to the bottom of a bottle of Tanqueray gin at fifteen years old. It led me to sordid places I never imagined I would enter. I found myself, more than once, stumbling around the mean streets of New York City in the wee hours of the morning, with the sun rising, looking for an open bar. I woke up next to strange bedfellows, unable to recall their names. Hunched over the porcelain goddess for hours, dry heaving, I promised God I would never drink again if he stopped the piercing pains shooting through my head, only to down a magnum of Pinot Grigio a few days later. The story I told myself drove me not just to addiction, but to failed relationships and a lot of heartbreak, during both my drunk years and the sober ones.

Generational family dysfunction underwrote the story of perceived but inaccurate feelings of apartness (always apart), bringing me to my knees, scraping and searching for meaning. It fancied the cape of emotional self-protection I wore, blinding me to my innate goodness. My despair ultimately exploded with enough desperation to reach out to those who could help me find meaning in the sorrow, courageous people willing to show me their wounds and how they healed. They offered me a way to meet and accept myself wholly, especially the parts I thought were bad or shameful, the same parts that needed healing.

These loving souls moved through a myriad of losses with me, such as getting sober, to living through a natural disaster, to choosing to move across the country, leaving precious friends and family behind. They brought me through the death of childhood innocence, encouraging me to say goodbye to old Amandas and to birth new ones. They walked beside me as I grieved wishes around my family of origin and the death of my beloved brother. They showed me how to mourn, how to bear the unbearable and then rise from the ashes. They journeyed with me from hopelessness to hopefulness, from hurting to healing, by guiding me toward unbridled self-worth. Then these beautiful people taught me how to build an eternal connection with myself, the universe, and those around me by loving and honoring every part of me, the admirable and the not-so-admirable. They taught me how to feel comfortable in my emotions to such an extent where I am safe to love and let go.

Why should you care about my story or read my suggestions? I'm not famous. I'm not mainstream. That's exactly why! Because I am you, a regular human dealing with common circumstances of life—fear, grief, joy, love—like you. My story of loss is written on your hearts, perhaps in a different language, but it's there, and my journey of powerful healing and self-love can be yours too.

These pages will show how my experiences and the lessons that followed are entwined with collective pain (your pain) and how mutual pain gives rise to compassion, the wellspring for trust, love, and connection. I use the word "collective" because I am you and you are me. We embody each other's marrow. What you do and say, the energy you emit into the ether, affects me and every living thing on this planet. Whether you are sitting at my kitchen table, driving your car along I-70, or living in Australia, we are one, constantly exchanging energy. This means we are both responsible for making sure our energy serves each other and humanity well.

I will suggest simple and effective ways of thinking and living to blend mind, body, and soul so they are no longer separate parts of you but work cohesively to serve you and those around you. Some of these concepts are documented elsewhere and can be found in both ancient and modern literature; some are new. It is critical to emphasize and reemphasize these principal laws of the universe; they cannot be reinforced enough in light of where humanity stands.

Threading these concepts together in a way that resonates on a personal as well as collective level, this book is an attempt to add fabric to your own tapestry and to inspire action—quietly or loudly, whichever suits your fancy. If you live these principles, which I am sure many of you do, wonderful! It's time to activate them universally and without conditions.

Nobody has this life figured out. I certainly do not. There is no summit of personal development. The grand scheme is too expansive for absolute understanding, and the mystery is what keeps us seeking, our brains and spirits alive and ever-evolving. However, we do need to develop meaning out of the sorrow and the joy, for our highest good and for the highest good of everything around us.

I place my story before you with the hope you will find comfort in a world that feels discomforting at times, to help you make sense of the insensible. You may begin to stitch together pieces of your life after reading about how I did so and feel empowered to bring forth the best version of yourself. Hopefully, your ambition, your pilot light of love, will burn so bright you will feel compelled to live it out loud and offer your gifts to the world—gifts that will heal both you and humanity.

To that I say … welcome home.

PROLOGUE

JULY 1985

A young girl peers over her shoulder to see what's happening on the far side of the playroom. "Everything is fine over here. Keep playing your game," says the babysitter lying on a couch with a five-year-old girl straddling his midsection. The two of them are playing a game of horsey. Bouncing her on his lap, the kindergarten-aged girl is smart enough and feels enough to know something is not right. Feeling icky, she squirms to get away. The man holds her there; he tells her she is okay and that they are having fun. He keeps bouncing. The rose garden she stares at outside the window turns from bright pink to black.

I am that kindergartener, a baby really, with pigtails and an eyelet shirt—a mother's sweet daughter, the picture of innocence. In that moment, the innocence vanishes and is replaced with a deep-seated feeling of "I am bad; I am dirty"—a story of shame. It settles in, taking root in the core of my being and begins to drive every self-destructive thought, emotion, and action for the next three decades of my life.

The Great Myth crystallizes in my head: The world is a dangerous place, and people cannot be trusted. Do not give of yourself fully because everyone will hurt you. Protect your heart and love a little less.

As untrue as The Great Myth was, I believed it.

Until one day the story ended.

1

THE CATALYST

2:23 P.M., MARCH 19, 2018

My phone rang on a sunny Monday afternoon. I know it was 2:23 p.m. because I looked at the clock, sensing this was a before-and-after moment, a colossal, life-defining point in time. I breathed deeply, gathered every morsel of courage, and slid the button to the right. Some things you just know, and this I knew: life would never be the same. Time, the great revealer, proved me correct.

My mother was on the other end of the line screaming repeatedly in horror and disbelief, "He's dead, Amanda. He's dead."

Trauma filled the room.

My childhood idol, my first friend, my brother, had died at forty-one years old after a twenty-five-year hell-ride with addiction. My mother's boy left this world lying on a sheetless mattress atop a cold, cement floor, inside a wooden shack situated some feet away from a drug-infested flop house. Clutching his chest as his tired heart failed him, his spirit rose to the heavens and he was set free.

After immediately booking a cross-country flight, I spent the following forty-five minutes wearing out the Victorian rug under the dining room table as I paced around like a caged squirrel. Phone in hand, I canceled appointments and called a few people with the horrific news. I yelled details about my children's spring break plans to my husband in the next room, who was experiencing shock similar to mine. But where he was unsure about how to comfort me, I was numb. I don't remember much after that. I don't even know who picked me up at the airport and dropped me at my mother's that night. The eerie familiarity of the numerous blackouts I had during my years of alcoholic drinking was upon me like a cloak of dread. Roughly twelve hours later, with "Off He Goes" by Pearl Jam playing, I started feeling and crying. My mom joined me on the couch, and I wept in her lap like a lost child. Then I passed out.

Jeremy was the one human being who knew what it was like to grow up in the yellow house on a dead-end street on the South Shore of Long Island, New York. He knew how to swing on the branches of the majestic weeping willow that grew beside the canal we lived on, as the warm summertime breeze danced across our young faces. He heard the same swarm of cicadas humming their mating call, distracting us from the green flies nipping at our ankles. Jeremy knew what it felt like to roll around our brown shag rug on Saturday mornings in 1985, building forts with the afghans our grandmother crocheted for us: Blankets carefully patched together, engineered to extend the entire length of the living room, with one square, brown snack table serving as the load-bearing beam. Talking Heads spinning on the family turntable as mom flipped pancakes in the kitchen. Dad tinkering with his prized Monte Carlo SS in the garage.

Jeremy was the boy who buckled my orange life preserver to board our speedboat for a thrilling ride through Zach's Bay, followed by a sun-drenched day at Short Beach. He knew the secret to catching jellyfish bare-handed at the end of our dock and the number of steps from our front door to the end of the stoop. Jeremy was the boy on the school bus I chased after when he left for his first day of kindergarten, sporting his platinum blond bowl haircut and infectious smile.

My brother Jason, eleven years my senior, shared in our childhood experiences as well. He lived with us from 1982 to 1988. Jason is my brother from my father's first marriage. I was two years old when he moved in and eight when he moved out. I have a lot of unforgettable memories about my time with Jason, like playing with our little, green plastic G.I. Joes and listening to his indistinguishable and entertaining impressions of Eddie Murphy and horses. (He once won twenty-five dollars for doing the best horse imitation at a local bar!) I will never forget Jason launching me overhead to fly five feet in the air into the above-ground swimming pool in our backyard, and me begging him to do it again. I looked up to him and loved when he spent time at our house, but Jason was not around for everything. Jeremy was the only person who shared completely in my youthful experiences—the highs and lows, day in and day out—from the laughs around the table as we savored Mom's Italian family tradition of Sunday sauce and meatballs to the tears of grief that accompanied the death of our grandparents.

He was my "Jermy," the excited little boy who on December 25 woke me at 4:00 a.m. shouting great tidings that Santa came. Jeremy was the one who flew up the basement stairs looking for help, propelled by sheer terror after watching me get electrified when my tiny fingers met the inside of an outlet. (My herculean stunt to unplug our ColecoVision in record time to avoid Freddy Krueger failed miserably.) Jeremy endured a million episodes of Mister Rogers' Neighborhood with me, as I rocked back and forth in my chair, sucking my thumb. He ran alongside me during Friday night games of Manhunt with the neighborhood kids, catching fireflies as we hunkered down in our hiding spots. He was the smart-aleck preteen who made fun of my nine-year-old gapped teeth (a Mack truck could fit through them, apparently) and the way I cried, like the wail of an ambulance siren.

Jeremy walked me into my first day of high school, a lowly freshman accompanied by her popular brother, a cool senior. He magically appeared around sixth period that same day when I was lost. I jokingly yelled his name, and he stepped out of the shadows as if he were expecting me to need him at that exact moment. He then led me to my next class, making sure to tell those we met along the way, especially the older boys, that I was his little sister.

Jeremy was my protector. He always had my back.

He knew my precise pain better than anyone else because he lived it too. He was the friend I leaned on when our parents told us they were divorcing. Jeremy was the person I cried to when our broken family, which had been broken for years, decided to break apart for good. He knew about the crazy family drama and the intense love. He felt the deceit and the confusion, the sensing

4

that something was wrong with our parents' marriage but not knowing what.

Jeremy sat next to me while Mom delivered the news of her breast cancer and told us of the surgery to follow that would hopefully save her life. His face fell, like mine did. He felt the fear that Mom might die, like I did, and the cold distance between our parents, like I did. He felt it all, just like me. Maybe he felt it even stronger, especially on the days when I rescued him from his own private nightmare, banging on his front door to make sure he showed up for a family celebration or pulling him out of bed, hungover, to join us for Thanksgiving dinner—or on the nights he called me, his system contaminated with a cocktail of substances and emotions running wild, bemoaning our deceased grandparents, irate over our parents' divorce.

Troubled as he was, Jeremy had a zest for life, a great sense of humor, and a heart of gold. He loved me like only an older brother could—roughing me up and wrestling me to the ground one minute, then draping his arm over my shoulder the next. We fought hard, and we loved hard. That's how the Italians do it!

Jeremy was the popular boy in school, the star athlete and student, the heartthrob. He was way cooler than me, and he had so much potential. He was the charismatic party animal that I aspired to be like but whose charm I couldn't quite match. Over the years, the charisma faded, the cool vanished, and people were baffled. The question I received most at his funeral was, "What happened?" The answer is I don't know. Addiction doesn't play favorites. It's an equal opportunity destroyer, visiting those from Park Avenue to the park bench, and everywhere in between.

I've carried a hole in my soul—an imperceptible, large, circle-shaped wound in my chest—for as long as I can remember, and in the year following Jeremy's death it broadened to encompass my entire body. His death stole a part of me. Suffering from acute grief like I had never known, I could physically feel something being removed, like the amputation of a vital organ: my heart. Most surreal, I was able to feel the deep hole within become filled with his spirit, taking up permanent residence in my being, like an out-of-body experience. It's hard to imagine, but we are closer now than when he was alive.

When Jeremy met his eternal spirit, I greeted my own. An odd encounter, it felt as if I had been granted access to the unseen. This overwhelming spiritual experience engulfed both my material and divine being as when the clouds part and the sun washes over the ocean, glistening and touching every molecule of water. Parts of me I didn't know existed awoke inside the shell of a human I had become, and it scared me half to death. The old Amanda was gone, replaced now with two strangers—one dead, the other very much alive. I didn't know what to do, how to feel, or who to be. I was stuck in limbo between two worlds, and although this wasn't the first time I felt this, it was more sweeping than before, stirring feelings I could not comprehend.

I've always had a sixth sense, but now I began to "know" things on a mystical level. I was able to sense how people felt and what they were going through by paying attention to my own feelings and experiences. Bits and pieces of my spiritual cognizance came together to serve those who allowed me to convey this newfound knowledge to them. This knowing was the cornerstone of the phenomenal tide of understanding that soon washed over me.

Phenomenal indeed, but I was mad as hell. How could Jeremy leave me like this? Why wouldn't he get the help he needed—the help he watched me wrangle when I reached the bottom of my alcoholism—the help my parents and I offered as we pulled him out of hotel rooms, chasing him down hallways as he ran from us in a state of drug-induced paranoia? Or when we took him to detox because we feared he would overdose, and he signed himself out against medical advice? Or the times we called 911, imploring the police to rescue him from his suicidal ideation? Why was he unable to accept help handed to him at the intervention our family and eight of his closest friends staged before he decided to move across the country—the move that took him away from his support in New York to Seattle, where he knew no one, delivering him to his final resting place? We entered his home desperate for him to seek treatment and left two hours later laughing and questioning why we were so worried. Succumbing to Jeremy's charm, we were once again convinced that we were overreacting and he had his ruthless drug addiction under control.

He claimed to have it under control until the time of his death. Jason happened to record their last conversation, a week before Jeremy took his last breath. It's a frightening account of how cunning this disease is and how torturous it is for the afflicted. I've listened to this recording only one and a half times because it breaks my heart more than anything else I have ever experienced.

The 6:30 a.m. call was thirty-eight minutes long and filled with bizarre highs and lows. It starts out jubilantly as Jeremy introduces his girlfriend to Jason, the both of them on speakerphone. They shoot the bull for a while, laughing and keeping it light until Jeremy, possibly because he is coming down from being high, starts to get low. Real low, as he explains what has been going on inside his chest for a couple of months: mini heart attacks piercing behind his sternum so strongly that he doubles over, unable to move as he chokes on his breath. It passes, he says, but he knows he needs to get to a doctor. Mom knows about these attacks and has been begging him to see a cardiologist, but he will not go because he knows what the doctor will say: he has to stop using drugs or he will die.

The disturbing truth is he will not see a doctor because he knows he will be handed a death sentence. He cannot stop using, and he knows deep in his soul his time is coming to an end. It's early March and he's known this truth for some time, definitely since the December prior, the last time he saw his eight-year-old daughter. She told me with confusion in her voice, "When I saw daddy last, he would not stop hugging me and crying. He was kneeling down, hugging me so tight and wouldn't let go." Her mother physically separated the skin-and-bones, gaunt, and distraught stranger from her child. He wouldn't let go because he knew he'd never see her again. The drugs had him. He knew this, yet he could not stop using. That is the power of addiction: Jeremy didn't choose drugs over his daughter. He was powerless to choose his daughter over drugs, to choose life over death.

A question we kick around in the rooms of recovery is "Why?" If I got sober, why couldn't he? If we grew up in the same house with the same parents and similar experiences, why could he not do what I did? Perhaps he had another mental illness (addiction is an

identifiable mental illness in the medical profession), a comorbid-
ity, which can make getting and staying sober more difficult. I have
witnessed dozens of people with anxiety, depression, and/or bipolar
disorder relapse for years on end. They struggle the most. I've also
witnessed scores of people with a dual diagnosis achieve long-term
sobriety. Maybe he didn't have another mental illness; maybe our
souls just have different paths.

It's been years, and I still have a hard time making heads or tails
of it. I'm driving, smiling, singing, and out of nowhere tears stream
down my face, utterances of grief come forth as I beg to know why
he left. We were supposed to celebrate our children's achievements
with one another, keep our childhood memories alive, and bury our
parents together. He was supposed to watch his daughter graduate
from college, walk her down the aisle, and teach her the wisdom
passed down to us from our parents. Thoughts like these enraged me
in the beginning. Now, they arrive—usually out of the blue—with
great stupor.

As insufferable as it was, my brother's death sent me on a journey
of debunking everything I knew to be true about life and love. His
passing set off a subconscious chain of existential angst, a deluge of
questions I had been yearning to answer my whole life, leading to
a spiritual awakening that shaped my identity and my heart in the
most incredible way. Jeremy's death delivered me to freedom.

I've heard some people die for others to live. If that is the case,
I'm in endless debt to my big bro, whose death shot me out of a spiritual cannon with the force of an atomic bomb.

The riddles of the ages captivate me. I've been seeking to discover some unknown truth since I first felt like something was not right, as early as I can remember. I was the one who constantly asked what we are doing here, what is the purpose of all this? There has to be more to this story, to this human experience. There has to be more fulfillment than running around, hands out, grabbing money and shiny things. There must be a purpose greater than waking up, going to work, paying bills, taking Johnny to soccer practice, throwing in a load of laundry, eating dinner, and doing it again the next day.

Something is amiss.

The purpose is to love: wholeheartedly, compassionately, and with trust. This is the simple answer to the complex mystery we have been trying to figure out for thousands of years. It's the calling our souls yearn to answer but we have a hard time answering. How do we answer it?

The Buddhist philosophy of impermanence seems reasonable in light of my questioning, the feeling that something is missing from the physical world, or at least missing from *my* physical world. The Buddha believed our souls are not of this earth. They are eternal, occupying a human being for a short time during each incarnation, and passing on to a new body in the next physical life. Our bodies act as vessels for spiritual growth. Since we are passing through, he believed we should not become too attached to materialism, including people. Not attaching to any earthly element as everlasting allows it to flow in and out with ease, without judgment and fear. It makes room for an open heart of love regardless of whatever loss may be coming down the pike.

I had heard of this principle before, but it wasn't until I was desperate enough to internalize it that I attempted to understand it. While searching for answers about how to grieve my beloved brother, I curiously wondered: How can I love someone and not be attached to the point of devastation when they leave? Aren't mothers supposed to be attached to their babies? Isn't that the point of life—to engage purely with others? And if so, how do I leave my emotions at the door? (We'll get to that.)

If the Buddhist belief of impermanence is valid, then it holds true that my purpose in life is to grow my soul into the most enlightened, loving spirit possible. This is because the everlasting part of me, the part that matters, is my soul. It's neither my waist size nor my bank account. It's my soul, and what matters is how lovingly and generously I share it with the people and the world around me.

The question is: can I attach in a healthy way knowing everything ends? Can I fully embrace love, joy, and connection with others knowing loss is inevitable? Can I nurture my relationship with myself as far as humanly and spiritually possible, propagating deeper relationships with others?

Can I love and trust myself enough to be all in?

This is the existential question that plagued me for years, but I had no answer.

2

NEW LIFE,
FRESH LOSS

Most of my life has been spent subconsciously sabotaging myself. I started the self-inflicted pain young. Cue the not one but two times I dropped a glass bottle and instinctually jumped on it, slicing open my little kid feet. Or the time Jeremy and I made the six-hundred-degree wood-burning stove in our living room home base during a game of tag, upon which I placed both of my six-year-old palms, leaving two tiny hands covered in blisters. That's to name a few. So, it's not surprising I spent what was at that time the latter half of my life, exactly thirteen of twenty-six years, self-harming my brain and body with substances, then suffering the consequences of chronic poor choices. Thirteen long, demoralizing years. And then it was over.

I called in sick to work. There was no DWI, no jail time. I didn't lose my children or get fired from my job. I simply called into work at two in the afternoon with a lame story that I had menstrual cramps and couldn't get out of bed. Well, I BlackBerried into work that I had menstrual cramps and couldn't get out of bed. The truth was, I was drunk from the night before. I emailed my supervisor and drank for another ten hours.

One-hundred-twenty-pound, twenty-six-year-old me drank wine for roughly twenty-eight hours the last time I got drunk. I came to the next morning with a pounding headache, dry mouth, and wreckage to clean up from the night before. Wreckage to which I was no stranger. There was always a mess to clean up. Who did I call at 3:00 a.m., and what on God's green earth did we talk about for a half hour? Did I start a fight with that person? How did I get home? Oh, there's my car in the driveway, luckily in one piece. Where did the bruises on my legs come from, and where are my shoes? This particular night was not unlike others, but something was different when I awoke from this particular debacle. Lyrics from a song played in my head, and I felt them like I had never felt lyrics before. Afraid I would die or kill someone else while driving in a blackout, as I often did, I was scared sober. I saw the light. I knew in that exact minute it was over.

For more than ten years, I was told I had a problem with alcohol; I knew I was an alcoholic as a teenager. It wasn't a secret—not to me or to anyone else who knew me. It wasn't normal to be the "designated drunk driver" at seventeen, driving with my hand over one eye so I'd stop seeing double while pulling over to vomit. Nor was it normal to raid my parents' liquor cabinet in the middle of the night, pour myself a glass of Wild Turkey, and light a cigarette off the gas stove (singeing my hair so badly that I walked the halls of high school for months with wispy bangs sticking straight into the air). My friends were not indulging in these late-night parties, and I knew I shouldn't treat myself this way. I didn't need a PhD to figure this one out. But knowledge is not enough when it comes to the disease of alcoholism, and I sure couldn't smart myself out from under the feelings of shame and low self-worth I carried.

It wasn't my mother's and father's pleas to stop drinking on the early mornings I plowed through the front door of my childhood home drunk, or my stint in outpatient rehab, that made me stop. It wasn't the night I spent Christmas alone at my college house in Albany, New York, because my dad kicked me out for strolling in at 7:00 a.m.—again. It wasn't the relationships I ruined or the times I could have caught a serious sexually transmitted disease that did the trick. So why, on this particular morning, on this random day, when I caused much less trouble than I had before, did I stop drinking? Was it divine intervention? I think so. I can't explain it any other way.

Every weekend for two months before my last drink I had a spiritual experience that stuck with me. The first one followed the death of one of my bosses, a rich, successful businesswoman. She fell and hit her head while holed up for weeks in her luxury apartment, suffering from depression. Smelling booze on her breath at 9:00 a.m. my first week on the job, I told myself if she can drink like that and be successful, so can I. I learned of her death while drunk myself. Curled up in the fetal position on the floor, I let out a scream. Then a voice from beyond whispered, "Amanda, you don't have to die this way." I was scared for my life, yes, but not scared enough to stop drinking for good, although I did go on the wagon.

Out to dinner with a college friend a few weeks later, intent on staying sober, I decided I could have one glass of red wine. Just one. (It was never just one. Thinking I can have just one is the deceptive lie of alcoholism.) At 5:00 a.m. and a few bottles later of whatever I could scrounge up in my friend's apartment, I found myself gallivanting around the gritty streets of New York City hunting for alcohol. Many young women were murdered in Manhattan at that time, and I was lucky to stay safe. The next day, my friend was pissed. She asked, "Why do you do this, knowing what happens?"

I told her, "I don't know, but I can't stop. I'm embarrassed and ashamed of myself."

She replied with a mix of frustration and compassion. "You shouldn't be ashamed of who you are; you should be ashamed of not getting help."

Bam! That hit me. A week later, I drank for the last time.

I don't know why that particular phrase at that particular time hit me so hard. All I know is I woke up the morning after my last bender knowing it was over, and it was.

I haven't had a drink since.

I believed it was over but cannot say with certainty I would have stopped for good if not for recovery. Alcoholism is a disease of the mind—a relentless obsession that does not lift until an alcoholic takes a drink. Then the physical compulsion, or allergy, kicks in.

That's the kind of alcoholic I am. Once it's in my head I have to drink, and when I start I cannot stop. There is the maintainer, and there is the binger. I am the binger. The morning I experienced a divine intervention I knew my binges were over, but due to the progressive mental illness aspect of alcoholism I may not have remained sober without making radical changes to my inner self and outer world— changes I didn't want to make but made anyway because my life depended on it.

Early recovery was a time of deep grief. I had to say goodbye to my life as I had been living it. I stopped going to familiar watering holes with familiar people. Friends stopped calling. Invitations to weekend barbeques ceased. Worst of all, I was mourning the death of my best friend, alcohol—the one true friend that never let me down. It gave me what I needed every time.

But I made new friends, and they were like me. The newcomers in the room at my first meeting felt afraid, alone, and just as faithless as I did. Humbled by our addiction, our pride was crushed with the admission that alcohol had us beat. We admitted our powerlessness over alcohol and sought comfort in this commonality. We found strength among one another to lift each other out of the dark pit of lonely, soul-stealing addiction—strength born after the leveling of pride and the birth of humility. No one was better or worse than anyone else; we were all battling the same demon. Our stories may have sounded different, but underneath each one was loss of something: our innocence, our families, our careers, our freedoms, ourselves.

I found the connection I searched for my whole life in the rooms of recovery. It was found in mutual pain and mutual hope.

I found my people.

Addiction and its cutting pain slice through the lives of the suffer-ers and those who love them with the force of a machete chop to a coconut. A powerful disease, addiction creates a sense of hope-lessness like no other disease does, leaving hearts broken in two. Mercifully, recovery is ripe with hopefulness and with life. I've seen the woman under the bridge become the CEO of a Fortune 500 company, the guy on the Harley cry in front of a crowded room because he got his children back, and the most hardened hearts soften with grace.

After a few weeks of attending meetings, I heard some of these stories and was so convinced that I jumped into recovery with both feet. Astonished to feel faith, I trusted if it worked for my ex-heroin addict, homeless friend who had been living in a treehouse before getting sober, it could work for me. Plus, the trees lining the park-way I drove down countless times seemed ultrasaturated with color, more dramatic. The fall leaves were illuminated in brighter shades of yellow and orange. The waves crashing at the shore I sat at hundreds of times before now had a heartbeat. The rushing wind whistled with spirit. The earth had a rhythm. I, too, felt a new rhythm. It fervently flowed through everyone I met, and I was attracted to it. I saw and felt people in a new, exciting light and needed what the recovered alcoholics in those rooms had.

When I was barely a week sober, a friend invited me to a meeting at six thirty the following morning. To his surprise, I showed up, and he told me I was going to be okay—I would make it.

I asked, "Why do you say that?"

He answered, "Because you're here and sober. When was the last time you were sober at six thirty on a Saturday morning? You're willing to go to any length. And kid, that's all you need."

I couldn't see who was speaking at the front of the room and began futzing with my seat, trying to gain a better view. My friend said, "You don't need to see. You just need to listen." And listen I did, to a bunch of pumped-up men and women hootin' and hollerin', excited to be there, to be alive. The pandemonium was mystifying. Sitting in a dank church basement way too early in the morning, I was in awe of the hundred people in this room who were sober and happy about it. I didn't know what the future held and I didn't care. I knew I was in the right place, with the right people. Anything was better than the way I had been living.

Early sobriety comes with suggestions from those who've had success in the program, and I was given many. The one suggestion I did not take was no new relationships in the first year. The purpose of not getting into a relationship in early recovery is to keep the focus on yourself, to learn who you are, and to avoid emotionally charged situations that could tempt you to relapse. The one-year mark is suggested not because after a year you're good to go, but because it typically takes a newcomer a year to go through the twelve steps. Completing the steps brings about a shift in perspective through what we in recovery call a psychic change. This change in psyche results in a better version of oneself, and we believe bringing that version to a relationship is the preferred method to start one.

I did not take this suggestion, and it did not work out well.

Eight months into my sobriety, on Easter Sunday 2007, my boyfriend didn't wake up. Mike was my first sober relationship, and we both experienced new, passionate feelings. I'm not sure if it was love or emotionality of early recovery, but we had a special connection. He was diagnosed with diabetes three months before his death. I was told he died in a diabetic coma; others say he relapsed and overdosed. Most likely both are true: an overdose put him into a diabetic coma.

I was at a restaurant eating dinner with my family when I got the call Mike was at the hospital, his heart not beating. The caller didn't say he had died, just that I should get there as soon as possible. Everything stood still in the vicinity of my physical being, but the room was spinning. I was an island unto myself, and the space around me rotated fast. There was a lack of oxygen. It was a strange sensation—one I had never experienced. Dissociated, I told the caller I'd be there when I finished dinner. I have a tendency to compartmentalize while in trauma, and that is what I did. I put Mike on his deathbed in a corner of my mind that I would tend to after my meal.

Snapping me out of delirium, my mother leaned over worriedly and said, "Honey, I think you should go." And I went. When I reached the emergency room, I said goodbye to Mike and to our blossoming romance. I was devastated.

I took time off work for the funeral and to process what happened. I attended recovery meetings and cried alone in my apartment. At the funeral, a sober friend asked if I wanted to join the No Matter What Club. I was confused but interested. She explained, "We don't drink, no matter what." I became a card-carrying member on the spot and did whatever was suggested from that moment on. It worked. The days passed, and I was staying sober.

That doesn't mean I was okay. I suffered my first emotional breakdown a month later while traveling from Fifty-Seventh Street to Fourteenth Street in Manhattan on a cloudy, brisk spring day. Before leaving the office, I received an email not meant for my eyes in which a higher-up made an insensitive but true observation about me. It was the straw that broke the camel's back. I boarded the subway for my work meeting upset, and by the time I exited the Union Square station I was beginning to melt down. A few blocks later, the floodgates opened. I was so distraught that not one, but two, passersby—at different times—stopped to ask if I was okay. (There are nice people in New York City. I promise!)

I assured them I was fine and took a seat on the steps of a random brownstone and continued bawling. Bereft, half an hour later, I gathered myself up and stepped melancholily from stoop to sidewalk. I headed back to the subway and sulked my way home to a lonely apartment. I spent the rest of that evening on my kitchen floor rocking back and forth, crying, gasping for air. Then I scraped myself up off the floor, shook it off, and went to a recovery meeting.

After that, life did what it does best … it went on. But a piece of me was left behind on that kitchen floor. A piece of me died that day.

Loss is often mischaracterized as losing a living, breathing creature, such as a person through death or divorce, or a pet. This may be the most painful kind of loss, but the most common form of loss is change.

Loss presents when saying goodbye to a season, during the comedown after a momentous celebration, or when a parent watches a child move on to the next stage of life. It happens when one evolves after a period of spiritual growth, when a person's identity braves an overhaul, no longer occupying the same wavelength as a friend or family member. Loss may befall us, rather achingly, after we set boundaries with loved ones. Any change, welcomed or not, brings loss. Moving to a new city or losing a job, even though a nicer neighborhood or better job awaits, involves a period of mourning. Grief ensues when we cannot accept the reality of those changes, regardless of viewing them as good or bad.

We experience loss when we refuse to let go of the old to embrace the new.

Heraclitus, a Greek philosopher and metaphysician alive in 500 BC, wrote, "Change is the only constant in life." That sounds like the backbone of impermanence to me. If life is change, then we are perpetually grieving one thing or another. Knowing this to be true, how wise is it to hold on to moments and people with a death grip? Probably not wise at all. You will invariably be left feeling abandoned and dispirited like I was: rocking, crying, and gasping for air on my kitchen floor.

3

SANDY &
THE MOVE

Unlike the onslaught of trauma from Mike's sudden and unexpected death, my second grief-induced breakdown took a few years to catch up with me.

It began on October 29, 2012, the night of Hurricane Sandy. A twelve-foot storm surge on the South Shore of Long Island flooded the beach town my new little family lived in, emptying much of the Atlantic Ocean into the streets of our barrier island. Our canary-colored stucco home collected seven feet of saltwater in the basement. The water rushed down our block with outrageous velocity, like Grand Canyon rapids at peak season, busting in the backdoor. Seaweed grazed the rafters. Small sea animals took up residence, seeking respite from the storm.

Immobilized briefly by the damage, my husband and I slowly surveyed the tremendous amount of material and emotional destruction we needed to clean up. We lost a car. We lost irreplaceable items from our childhoods and from our baby daughter's first year of life. We lost memories. I sat on the porch peeling wet photos out of albums, reluctantly deciding which ones to rinse off to keep and which ones to toss. Each picture thrown in the garbage felt like it was taking a piece of myself with it.

Wedding china and the porcelain doll that once sat on the shelf in my childhood bedroom floated in the oil-infested water. Loyal friends came down to the beach to help us. They hopped into the deep, grimy seawater and passed objects through a conga line, up and out of the tiny basement windows. Other people helped sort through the remnants of our lives scattered about the property, trying to save whatever they could. Items were placed into the bleach bucket, into the clean water bucket, bleach once more, clean water again, and laid on a tarp or hung on a line. That was the protocol. It took five weeks, thirty-five days from sunrise to sunset, but my husband managed to get it done and to salvage what he could. I still shudder when pulling out the special cake plate for birthday celebrations and see the line of super glue holding together a broken memory.

Friends and neighbors weren't as lucky. People lost their homes, schools floated off their foundations, and businesses were boarded up. Helpful Samaritans drove down our suburban street, once home to colorful garden beds lining the walk, now filled with mud and debris, handing out bottled water and cans of Chef Boyardee. We consorted with our kind neighbors, sharing gas for our generators. Living through a natural disaster is not the same as watching a Red

Cross infomercial. It was a catastrophic and traumatic event that mutated our sense of security in the community we loved. If you've experienced one, you know what I mean.

The evening of the storm, my downtrodden father, who had lived through a few major hurricanes in his waterfront home, told me he had to abandon ship. He gave it the good fight. Once he realized Mother Nature was not holding back, he put on his rubber boots and waded through the waist-high water down the driveway and up the block to safety. He had never left before. I knew this was bad, not because he had to leave, but because of the shell-shocked tone of his voice as he conveyed the awful news to me on the other end of the line.

I called my husband, who was guarding our house with our dog and upstairs tenants, but couldn't reach him. Sheltered at my mother's apartment with my ten-month-old daughter, safe but horrified, I pulled out the United States map and pointed to the middle of the country. Kansas. I thought it might be a big leap for this New Yorker to relocate to Kansas so I began scouting out other inland states. Nothing tickled my fancy. Then I remembered Carole, my spiritual mentor and confidante who had attended a festival in Estes Park, Colorado, that summer. She came back raving about it (aside from her altitude sickness). I trusted her instincts. So, I looked left of Kansas and said to myself: *We are moving to Colorado.* I had quietly been considering moving from the East Coast for a while. Sandy blessed me with a knowing that it was time to go.

We moved from New York to Colorful Colorado in May 2015. In a foreign land, with no friends or family to walk me through the awkward feelings a change like moving brings, I was lost.

Nine years sober, I couldn't connect to the recovery community in our new town and didn't understand why. I was attending lots of meetings, acting as secretary of a group and treasurer for another, yet I couldn't find my footing like I had in New York. Pulling over to the side of the road on my way home from a meeting one night, I sobbed frantically because I missed my sober family, especially Carole, and I feared for my sobriety.

My personal relationships were suffering as well. Close bonds with friends and relatives were strained; they were upset we chose to move so far away. They could not understand why we would rather be in Colorado and not with them, why we would choose to miss births of babies, graduations, and holidays. They felt abandoned by us. It was a sad time in all our lives.

With no outline for the human-constructed role I was supposed to settle into, and with little support, I had no idea who I was. Unfamiliar with the social norms of our new town, I questioned every action, wondering if it was appropriate. After a year of muscling through, I hit the wall of mental and emotional well-being, big time. My secure New York identity dissolved, and I was left highly unsettled. Walking through a newly developed supermarket, I became disoriented because I could not find the milk. Humans are creatures of habit because habit provides comfort. Not knowing where the refrigerated dairy case was located was the minor situation that left me majorly disturbed. My security blanket was ripped off and my comfort stripped away right there in aisle four. Wandering around slightly deranged, I was lost in a labyrinth of produce and frozen food, in a labyrinth of my mind.

My second emotional breakdown was developing at the same time everyone started dying. Our family mourned the loss of five beautiful souls inside three years: Aunt Rosie and Aunt Louise (Mom's two sisters); my cousin Kim, so close to me that she was a bridesmaid in my wedding; my mother's first cousin Linda, the definition of selfless love; and Jeremy, the last to end the procession. Four out of five deaths were sudden and unexpected. With each loss, emotional and physical, another part of my identity burrowed further into the soil of my hollow being, grief ignored.

Suffering from a self-diagnosed adjustment disorder (breakdown in aisle four ... ahem) and later professionally diagnosed with generalized anxiety disorder, I also felt stifled in a marriage that looked good on the outside but was falling apart behind closed doors. The oppressive emotions took over, and an argument with a friend left me on the floor (this time the bedroom floor) in agony, guttural screams escaping from my mouth. The pain I was expelling held the part of me that felt comfortable knowing my place—how and when to act. It was filled with behavioral expectations I had grown to know well and extreme fear that I wouldn't fit in because I didn't know who I was supposed to be. Once it was released, I reassembled the pieces that were left and began restructuring my identity based on who I am, not on whom I should be according to the norms where I was living or who I spent my time with. The pieces I pulled together, one by one as I listlessly gathered myself up off the floor, became the foundation of the woman of worth I am today.

In the year leading to this crisis, an insightful friend suggested I devise a *personal* meditation practice. She insisted it would help me. During my adolescent years of meditation, I could not consistently settle my mind long enough to affix a regular routine in place. I sat for three minutes—"while the coffee drops" as Carole suggested—but my mind raced and I'd find something else to do. I would wash the one dish in the sink, jot down an item to buy at the grocery store, scrub the toilet—anything to not sit with my thoughts. I had resisted the feelings that might come up for fear I could not handle them. But the urge to try lingered and developed into a solid, daily practice years later. In despair and desperate for peace, I did whatever I was told to do.

As they say, desperate times call for desperate measures.

Rising before the sun at 5:30 a.m., I padded downstairs to my new, peculiar kitchen where everything felt curious. I lit a candle. Sitting alone in the dark, I reached for a stimulating passage from a daily meditation book, closed my eyes, and asked my Higher Power to enter my heart. I breathed big belly breaths, sticking my stomach out as far as I could to engage the vagus nerve, enhancing feelings of tranquility.

The vagus nerve runs from the brain to the abdomen. When stimulated through controlled, deep breathing, the vagus nerve activates the parasympathetic nervous system, releasing neurotransmitters. These neurotransmitters signal the brain to relax. Heart rate and blood pressure decrease, and the digestive tract calms. This is known as a change in vagal tone. With a placid vagal tone, feeling peaceful, I consciously withdrew my will and gave permission for something else to steer the ship.

I sat, and waited, and waited.

Then the magic happened. I envisioned an amber glow in the shape of a human walking toward me, arms outstretched, casting beams of light. The beautiful, warm rays extended from his/her/its/their (doesn't matter what you call it since it's energy) hands and began to permeate my heart. It was filling the gaping hole I carried my entire life. This figure was my Higher Power, intimately showering me with love.

Tears arrived, flooding the empty vessel that sat at that table. I began to be filled with holy, divine warmth and acceptance. I remembered a suggestion from Carole. She painted a picture for me: my Higher Power picking me up and swinging me around like a child while telling me it loves me. I placed that in my vision and was inundated with comfort, joy, and a feeling of unrestricted love. I knew there was nothing I could do, or not do, that could limit this love. It was glorious.

I let the pain out, and was completely humbled. Holding nothing back, I was raw, naked, and open to what this powerful force was doing with me. Basking in the light, I was connected to something greater than myself more deeply in that moment than in the prior nine years I had been searching. It was healing, for sure. Most powerfully, it cracked open the door of willingness to see, hear, feel, and know whatever I needed for my voyage toward becoming the highest version of myself.

This overpowering love gravitated from out there to deep inside. It began externally, moved to the periphery, then reached my soul. I caught glimpses of unadulterated love for myself. The healing tears kept flowing. I knew I was changing. I was becoming love. The seeds planted years before sprouted. Nothing grows without water, and my tears were the essential element in the metamorphosis of my spirit. Afterward, I wrote about it in my journal at great length.

It never ceases to amaze me what happens when I put pen to paper. The rapid transfiguration is incredible. The part of me that hides under pretense emerges. I begin with what is often a skewed perception driven by fear and conclude with the Holy Spirit's wise direction. Lifted out of my often-sick head space, I travel to a clearer and cleaner version of myself. It feels so good that I can't wait to journal again.

Over months of meditating and journaling on a daily basis, my cup began to fill quickly. I began to understand the best way to go in and through suffering is to give it meaning. First we must feel the pain, then seek the lesson and focus on that. This helps us embrace and accept the unavoidable trials of life. The meaning of this particular trial was to create a new identity based on authenticity. At this awareness, my self-worth grew in leaps and bounds. Entering into a trustworthy partnership with my Higher Power, I listened intently for messages about how to live authentically and lovingly. I started to believe in my power to send this love to you; it felt too big, beautiful, and special to keep for myself.

Years before this experience, my New York therapist, Colleen, told me to visualize people all over the planet holding hands, sending love to one another. I recalled this vision, imagining a big circle of the whole human family. I invited my Higher Power's light in to power this Ring of Love. I sent feelings and thoughts of love and connection to you. Energetically entering into a loving-kindness partnership with the rest of the world, I became one with you and felt safe in our collective vibrations. I remained in silent partnership for as long as my mind allowed, gaining guidance for how to live peacefully in oneness.

I listened hard and felt the connection, challenging myself to *be* love for as long as possible. I would not allow myself to move to another feeling when it became uncomfortable. I began to absorb love, then transmit it. This energy is the nucleus of healing on both a personal and collective level, and by allowing it to take control of me, I knew I was healing the world and myself.

These daily morning meditation sessions of authenticity, self-worth, love, and oneness came to a close as the sun rose over my cul-de-sac, splashing rays of vivid pink and orange across my monochromatic living room, once a blank slate, now filled with color.

I blew out the candle, thanked whatever … whomever … was granting me this loving guidance, and moved on with my day, holding hands with you.

4

EMBRACE
THE PAIN

O
ur society views strength as the ability to tolerate emotional pain. We are taught to keep on keeping on no matter how bad we feel. Vulnerability with emotions is the real strength. Staring down pain takes courage and audacity, and the valor is in the healing. This misconception of strength, a.k.a. soldiering on while suppressing emotions passed down through generations, is at the heart of most pain and dysfunction.

Dysfunction is relative and subjective; what is considered dysfunctional today may not have been to our ancestors. Perhaps some hurtful behaviors passed on were done so in the name of survival. Did suppressing emotion keep our elders alive?

Centuries ago, in a disease-rampant civilization, mother didn't have time for bedtime stories and cuddles as she was working hard to keep eight children fed, clean, and healthy. Affection was sacrificed in exchange for existence. And she certainly couldn't allow herself to feel deep grief, the kind necessary for healing. Should she be consumed by pain, she may not be able to keep those kids in good health. This idea is especially valid for men. Shrieking in terror while preparing to kill an enormous buffalo to feed a family is not conducive to staying alive.

Although some manners of conduct may have been purposeful in the past, dysfunctional behaviors do not serve us well today and are being challenged. The younger generations are not complying with the old adage "It's always been done this way." We feel a pull to reinvent the antiquated systems and messages passed down. These tired concepts do not work anymore. Society is changing; a New Earth is emerging in which open-mindedness and connection are necessities, not luxuries. Those who break the chain of generational dysfunction are commissioned with expressing themselves earnestly, honestly, and with passion wherever and whenever they feel moved to—most notably, within our families.

Generational family dysfunction is the source of the chaotic society we live in. Pain spills out our front doors and inundates communities with turbulent fallout from untreated familial trauma and long-lived resentments.

Circumventing pain with the hope it will miraculously vanish is the first distorted notion that needs to go. This pervasive, life-taking fallacy—this pack of self-protective lies used to avoid facing wounds—has taken root in some families stronger than a thousand-year-old oak tree. Withstanding the test of time, emotional self-protection has engrained itself so deeply it dominates interactions, sometimes quite deceptively and involuntarily. Unaddressed and unhealed, repressed feelings rise up and come out sideways, forcing the communicators to succumb to manipulative tactics like gaslighting, triangulation, and negative sarcasm to obscure their hurt, often against their will. Willful or not, the recipients are left confused and sore.

We must write about it and talk about it. We must share openly with those who understand and care: therapists, friends, and family members who can help decipher the hurtful behaviors. Most importantly, we must become aware of our own deceptive need to emotionally self-protect or we will pass it on, continuing to harm ourselves, our families, and society. Some harm may be deadly.

Shutting down emotions results in disease in many forms: anxiety; depression; substance abuse; addiction to gambling, sex, food, and spending; workaholism; high blood pressure; and suicide. Mental, emotional, spiritual, and physical pain are our body's built-in check engine lights and, if ignored, pain breaks us down. Alternatively, healthy emotional responses to pain positively affect the body. A healthy response means you appraise the level of pain present and select a balanced, honest approach. You choose to feel your feelings. By choosing to feel your feelings, you hold the power to reduce disease not only in yourself, but in the people around you, such as your children. At ease, you become comfortable sharing your feelings with your children, which helps them process their own and brings them peace. Incredibly, this healing may pass on cellularly to future generations; a theory that is becoming widely accepted as science confirms the imprint of emotional health on your DNA.

I am here to report happily and confidently that feeling your feelings will not kill you. Choosing not to feel your feelings will, in fact, kill you. It may be a slow, insidious death, but the grim reaper named "I-don't-want-to-feel-that-so-I-will-pretend-it's-not-happening" will eventually call your number.

So feel it. Embrace the pain, and break the chains of generational family dysfunction. Your heart and soul have the right to be free and healthy.

I surmise I've had many past lives. Those lives provided the lessons and emotional evolution needed to face the harrowing experiences of this lifetime. They have gifted me with the ability to grow through discomfort.

Pain today is not payment for bad deeds in a previous life. It's not punishment for sins of the past. It doesn't work like that. At least I don't think it works like that. My current life experience is an offering from my Higher Self as a chance to free my soul. I do this by facing my brokenness and growing as close to whole as possible.

I believe we are born whole, with a strong connection to divinity. The first rupture to our wholeness is when we realize we have been separated from the divine. Not truly separated, as spiritual connection can never be severed, yet there is a definitive feeling of apartness. This is our first fracture. (I believe this happens shortly after birth.) Life continues to break us down, providing opportunities to understand lessons we agreed to learn when spiritually whole, between lives. After a slew of painful life events, we hit a crescendo of lament. We break, then spend the rest of our time on earth growing back toward wholeness. We grow by healing wounds in an attempt to reach the full unification of our soul, which is only possible upon returning to the light. Still, we aspire to put our pieces back together as best we can. This is part of our soul's excursion, and these wounds are as they should be. The powerful loss compels us to seek enlightenment, to grow closer to whole, closer to spirit.

Broken does not imply there is something wrong with you. It simply means the shards of your whole self that shatter due to painful events need to be mended. The fracturing yields potential to grow toward wholeness.

Kintsugi is a Japanese art form that finds beauty in brokenness. Broken pieces of pottery are made whole again by sealing the sections together with lacquer mixed with gold powder. The cracks represent the piece's wounds, and the wounds are what give the ameliorated bowl or plate meaning. Your wounds give your life meaning. They remind you of where you don't want to return to and how far you've come. They reveal your pain *and* your growth.

Some scars will never be smoothed over. Once blemished, you will never be exactly the same. That is the blessing. The change is the blessing! It's your new life: the kintsugi of your soul. It's the story of the broken piece of pottery—better for having been wounded, and the tarnishing is the gift. You're the one who gets to write a new story after the brokenness—a past that holds new meaning and a future based in freedom.

It's not about erasing your painful past. It's about transforming hurt into health, broken into whole. And that, my friend, is the golden nugget, the gem of all gemstones.

I often wonder what I did to deserve such agonizing heartbreak. Why me? Where does the pain come from, and why do some of us receive an extra helping of emotional assault?

Is it the result of nature or nurture? Books are written, lectures are given, and longitudinal studies are conducted on the subject. The answer is that it's both. Nurture may be the indicator of your pain, but the problem was with you from birth—that's the nature part. The nurturing either made the problem harder to define and solve or availed an effective strategy to deal with it. Whether your family added to or reduced your trouble, you were still going to experience that particular trouble. The warmest caretaker in the world could not protect you from the lessons your soul has planned for you.

My soul chose this life and the people in it for its evolution. The universe is giving me exactly what I need, when I need it—especially the pain. The idea we choose our loss or pain is a hard pill to swallow when some of us have suffered unfathomable abuse and tragedy. Why would you choose that? The hard truth is most of your lessons were planned before returning to Earth. Skipping the easy path, our souls decided to go through whatever pain we must to evolve. Still, this doesn't mean we chose the details of those tragedies.

I don't believe specific events are premeditated, but lessons are, and your personalized education plan is determined by your soul's desire to grow. Life is a collaboration of your soul contract (agreed-upon lessons) and your choices, your free will. Both ideas are true: individual agency and destiny. This means the decisions you make will lead to the learning one way or another. You can avoid the painful lessons for a while, but if your soul is intent on gaining knowledge from the jagged roads of life (like the majority of souls alive today), you will find yourself there eventually.

Tough times are not your Higher Power's fault. Even though this benevolent energy nudges us toward good choices, which often result in good outcomes, it does not protect us from bad things happening. Nor is our Higher Power solely responsible for the good. This force does not take people from us, arrange car accidents, provide the winning lottery ticket, or supply us with parking spaces. It is not a puppet master, bestowing gifts or punishing with pain based on what we are doing or not doing. Outcomes are not the result of my belief in God or how often I pray. Neither are my thoughts always responsible for the way the universe endows its charms and its bedevilments upon me. Sometimes they are; sometimes they aren't.

Other people's manifestations also affect my life. I'm not responsible for anyone else's soul lessons or choices, only my own, but I agreed to be close to certain people to learn from them. My brother's life was the effect of lessons he needed to learn, and my family is experiencing our own lessons because our souls are intertwined. Although Jeremy's death is no one's fault but his own, we have work to heal from it, work we agreed to do before this incarnation and may not have been able to do without my brother dying. Maybe we could have learned the same lesson another way; I'm not sure. Nevertheless, Jeremy's journey presented us with learning our souls desired regardless of the circumstance that brought us to it.

My life experience is a combination of my energy with my Higher Power's energy and the energy of those around me. Positive alignment of these energies—continually, purposefully, and with focused intent—brings good outcomes. And the bad stuff? My negative thought patterns create most of it but not all. Every occurrence is not governed by the same law, but every event can be used as an opportunity for growth—to learn or to change. (With this perspective, there are no bad events, just difficulty—sometimes extreme difficulty.) This attitude helps me to not blame, shame, or judge myself, others, or my Higher Power when pain rains down.

We can make assumptions why good and bad things happen, but being mortal, we will never truly know. The mystery of faith suggests we aren't supposed to know. We are supposed to trust through the joy and the pain, constantly seeking the lesson.

I know for sure that whatever is supplying me with my personal experience is giving me a touch more than I can handle. (Okay, maybe a lot more than I can handle!) This is so I rely on something greater than myself to help me through hard times, and each time I do, I become more enlightened. Forced to seek guidance, I advance the evolution of my soul. Besides, if I could handle it, I would have already ascended into the spiritual bliss of the heavens having it all figured out, never to return.

But here I am and here you are, still searching for answers in the game of life.

Time does not heal wounds. It teaches us to manage wounds. We manage wounds by feeling our pain as we pursue resilience to rise. Over time, you rise. Trust the magic of time to restore your resilience after loss.

Resilience is part of the human spirit and is inside us, like our connection to divinity. There is no way you do not possess resilience, but your belief system and lack of patience may convince you otherwise. Ask yourself if your limiting beliefs are holding you back from flexing your resiliency? If so, peel away the layers of defeatist messages you tell yourself, the loud whisper convincing you the pain is too great to heal and because it's taking so long it will never happen. Replace these lies with authoritative messages of resilience, trust, and patience, some of which are found in nature.

In May, the forest of scrub oaks in my yard blooms with vibrant, life-affirming green leaves. In October, the leaves die. Shedding leaves, the tree preserves energy to stay alive over the long winter. Branches break off during vicious storms and regenerate months later, as do new, hardy leaves the following May.

Have you risked breaking apart to become stronger? Do you trust your spirit to regenerate with more vibrancy? Have you given yourself time to heal? Think of your most challenging years of life. Did you come out of them with more skepticism and fear, walled off from the joy of living, or did you use the pain and the time to strengthen your resilience?

You grew stronger? Good. Resilience looks great on you! It shines out through your eyes and lights the world with hope and inspiration. Your example of resilience helps your depressed friend get out of bed. It cheers on your ailing parents when they cannot muster the strength to make their own funeral arrangements. It motivates your children to sincerely congratulate their opponent on a win they desperately wanted for themselves.

Communication with the universe lights the long path toward

resilience. This path, packed with wisdom, will guide you if you are open to it and practice patience. Over time, wisdom mutates pain into strength. Messages of resilience rush in to dispel despair and refresh your spirit. You only need to wait, notice the messages upon arrival, and become willing to breathe in truth and breathe out pain. Breathe in strength, new life, wisdom. Inhale deeply through the nose, sticking out the belly to engage the vagus nerve. Exhale slowly.

Breathe out despair, defeat, or grief.

5

THE CURTAIN

Three months after Jeremy met his maker, I convinced myself I was getting better, that my grief was subsiding. I knew it was quick but felt assured the inner work I completed over the previous twelve years in recovery meant my superhuman coping skills kicked in and I was healed.

I wasn't healed. I just decided I was done with the sadness. I didn't want to feel it anymore. Tapping into whatever capacity I had to live, I marshalled my will and picked myself up from a puddle of tears. It was June, my favorite time of year, and I wanted to be in the flow. Plastering a smile on my face, I jumped back into life and service work with my church and recovery community. The brain is astounding. It will go far and wide for self-preservation, and that is exactly what mine did. My emotional and mental states were in such disarray I could not foretell the truth soon to catch up with me.

Two months later, while at Pearl Jam's Home Shows in Seattle, reality smashed my comfortable denial like a sledgehammer to a sheet of ice. I took a five-day trip with one of my closest sober sisters to see our favorite band play two nights in their hometown.

My first Pearl Jam concert was with Jeremy in 1996. Sixteen years old, I begged my parents to let me go. After I tormented them for days, they allowed me to board a Greyhound bus headed for upstate New York, where Jeremy was a freshman in college. I rode the bus for eight hours, then we drove four more hours to Buffalo. He and his friends ditched me to sneak into the mosh pit of sweaty grunge fans, and I was left to watch the show alone. Mesmerized by the energy of the band and the intensity of the crowd, I felt connected to people in a way I had never felt connected before. It was the beginning of a lifelong obsession with Pearl Jam. Jeremy and I went to other PJ concerts together over the years and frequently sent videos and lyrics to each other; their music bonded us. My brother will always be my best Pearl Jam buddy.

The Home Shows years later pulled back the curtain, the thick window dressing I was hiding behind. The existential questions I wondered about all my life hit me and hit hard.

Sleeping on the sidewalk to get near the "rail" (roughly thirty feet from the stage), I and a group of fellow die-hard fans spent hours upon hours in line, bonding over our love for this band. There was an emotional and spiritual connection present, a shared intimacy created by a common thread of loss. We were all grieving something: loved ones, relationships, childhoods, wishes. Pushing emotional boundaries to find our place among one another's pain, we lowered our guards. We saw each other's suffering as reflections of our own in the mirrors we held up.

Nineties grunge music screamed resonantly. It not only gave voice to teen angst but spoke to trauma within the walls of our homes. The dark tones demonstrated our anguish, and the pain-filled, expressive lyrics put language to feelings that otherwise eluded us. Converging on the sidewalk, sharing our pain and our excitement with one another, we entered a sacred space the likes of which only our street-mates could understand. We were healing. That's the power of music mixed with pain: it heals.

Chalk it up to divine timing; greater forces put this group of souls together for lessons we needed to learn. I now understand my extreme fandom. My affective connection to Pearl Jam's music had been leading me here to heal. Because of my acute grief and the collective energy, I was deeply connected to spirit and moved within at the shows and with the people I met. I broke down during the song "Jeremy," and strangers who were not strangers at all put their hands on me to support me, to love on me. It was one of the most beautiful expressions of humanity I've personally experienced.

Along with the grief and the healing, there was a huge shift taking place—an awakening—a rearrangement of thoughts, feelings, and emotions for which I was not prepared. I felt alive, similar to early recovery but this time I was *really* alive. My senses were in peak condition, all six of them. In tune with myself and others and transported to a higher vibration, I was on top of the world and felt more authentic among these people than ever before. I thought of my husband, my life back in Colorado, and how detached I felt. Why was my pulse quickened, my mind and heart open, and my pain on the table with this group of strangers and not at home? I loved my family. So why did I feel like I had been living in black and white with a touch of gray fitfully strewn in, and now a box of vibrant markers splayed out in front of me?

Between minutes two and three of "Better Man," I realized I turn the dial when that song plays on the radio, telling myself it's overplayed and I'm tired of hearing it. During the chorus of a song I've heard a million times, I got honest about why I do that. "She lies and says she's in love with him. Can't find a better man."[1] I decided that marrying my husband was intentional, a premeditated decision, not a propulsion due to chemistry. He would provide me with security. He was good for my survival. Grounded in recovery at eleven years sober compared to my one when we met, I believed he would keep me on the right path. Plus, he was successful, and he chose me! A picky man, I could not comprehend why he chose me; I felt lucky.

In that moment, I decided I didn't love my husband, that I never loved my husband.

These thoughts rushed in at the same time I experienced a mind-blowing magnetic pull toward one person in particular, a spiritual attraction I could not wrap my head around. Experiencing the ultimate blindsiding, I saw and felt something I never saw or felt before. Disturbed with unbearable anxiety, I was shocked and stunned by these emotions. Out of my mind with a deep feeling of connection overshadowed by panic, I didn't know what to think or what to do. Why did I feel seen by someone I just met and not with the man I was with for years? How could this person understand my pain and meet an indefinable emotional need I didn't even know I had?

With eyes wide open, I wondered if I was watching a horror flick or a romantic drama as the state of my marriage came into view: I was not happy and hadn't been for years. It was time to look behind the heavy curtain and face these disquieting emotions. Out of hiding places and unable to run from it any longer, I was forced to pry open the curtain I had shut tight so no truth would spill out—the truth that I was desperately trying to avoid looking at. My unfulfilling yet acceptable marriage became unacceptable, and I could not live with this knowing, and this pain, for one more day.

My spirit, my higher consciousness, was heralding me to heal, and it would not take no for an answer. I had a sneaking suspicion that Jeremy, orchestrating from the super-unknown, had something to do with this. Our parents' divorce strummed in my head as I heard the strings of history replay themselves.

Enter breakdown number three: an emotional uproar that rendered debilitating depression and anxiety—the kind I heard about and tried to support others through but never knew myself. I couldn't understand why I felt this way. Life was pretty good, and I should have been happy and grateful. Why wasn't I? This epiphany brought me not to my knees, but straight to the floor. (This makes three floors I have hit: the kitchen, the bedroom, and now the bathroom floor for the trifecta!)

Crouched down, forlorn, I cried out in bewilderment. Sent down into a black hole of confusion and heavy sadness, I was filled with paralyzing fear. I was so shaken I barely ate for the following five weeks; I hardly slept. Some called it the grieving process; others suggested bipolar disorder. I hadn't exhibited bipolar symptoms so I dismissed that. Others saw it as a spiritual awakening. I chose what was behind door number three.

Disclosing my deepest pain and my deepest fear quenched my

thirst for the part of me that was missing my whole life—the most meaningful part.

Sometimes we must find ourselves in the most conundrumous (not a word but I like it) of situations to become desperate enough to challenge long-held beliefs, to grow. Heading toward divorce was my height of desperation. I'm talking Empire State Building height. With fear gripping to protect me, I found myself on the observation deck of the greatest conundrum I had ever known. I had two choices: I could call upon my bravery, peer over the edge, and look at why divorce was on the table. Or I could hide in some hidden shaft of the structure I built around me to shield me from the painful truth.

Filled with crippling fear, I decided to take a look.

Periodically, while meditating, I hear the words from Proverbs 3:25, "Be not afraid." This phrase does not suggest fearlessness. It means I do not allow fear to dictate my actions or become terrified to the point that I cannot act. This is when I summon bravery or am graced with it, whichever way you want to look at it. Strengthened by bravery mixed with fear, I recognize the fear, put it in perspective, and find the guts to take action. After a while, the fear subsides but never disappears. I'm grateful fear never abandons me. It's my inner benchmark indicating there is work to be done, my messenger telling me what I have to do.

Fear's good friends, anxiety and confusion, couple up powerfully to serve me. Anxiety hustles, trying to convince me to make a move and to make it now. Luckily, confusion steps in, inhibiting my ability to move forward. Gifting me with time to contemplate the truth of the situation, fear stills me long enough to find perspective. Healthy choices emerge, and I am free to make a thoughtful decision that helps me instead of one that hurts. Some days I trust the fear, some days I don't, but I always know it's there for a reason.

Facing the end of my marriage thrust me into the shadow of fear, and moving forward within that fear walked me into the light of faith. But I didn't walk into faith and stay there. I vacillated between fear and faith many times before I reached steady comfort. Vacillating between fear and faith, between smallness and greatness, is necessary for the quest toward personal freedom. Greatness reveals the next step in my healing process, and smallness agitates, pushing me into willingness to take that step.

I often ask myself if I would rather live with contented mediocrity or take the risk for greatness. If I want to become a more loving, courageous, and emotionally generous version of myself, how honest am I willing to get and how much pain am I willing to endure? If I want greatness more often than smallness, what will I risk to seize it?

Comfort? Predictability? The easy way out? Yes, yes, and yes.

I could not fathom this was happening in my marriage but knew I wanted better. By this time in sobriety, my self-worth had grown to a point when I felt safe to put on boxing gloves and meet my fear in the parking lot, where I've been told by my fellows in recovery she's waiting for me, doing push-ups! I was ready to courageously square off with myself.

I had been seeing Tracy, my therapist, for five months to help me cope with Jeremy's death. Now we had a different agenda. I marched into her office brazenly, denial drumming through my head; its beat thumped in my ears and pounded on my heart. I told her I wanted it all, that I was afraid of missing out on love if I didn't follow what I felt at the concert. She told me I could have it all. I didn't believe her because I never felt that kind of connection with any other human and I would not accept life unfulfilled on any level. I deserved more and didn't feel bad for wanting more.

Tracy was patient with me as she showed me the truth about the story I had been telling myself my entire life. It coincided with a phone call I had with an old friend a few days after the mysterious Seattle event. My friend brought to my attention that I was never "into" the people I was romantically involved with. They always cared more deeply for me than I did for them. I had to admit this was true, and so I took a hard look at it. The same friend told me years prior to this conversation that I was constantly preparing for the worst. Her two accurate observations go hand in hand: I didn't allow myself to be all in with romantic partners, keeping happiness out of reach for fear of getting hurt. I chose to enter relationships in which true partnership was unattainable. I spotted the walking wounded, the emotionally unavailable, and decided *That's my guy!* And when I met the well-adjusted, nice guy … well, he wasn't for me. Neither the wounded nor the well could make me happy.

The overarching theme about relationships passed down through generations in my family is that it's better to love a little less. That way, I will not be left in pieces when someone leaves or hurts me, and they will. I learned the people closest to me cannot be trusted and the world is an unsafe place. Taking those messages to heart, I kept myself separate from a devoted, vulnerable connection. I believed a pure, reciprocal, loving relationship was not obtainable, and happy families don't exist.

I'd see joyful couples and families and stare in disbelief and judgment. Quietly accusing them of lacking authenticity, I assumed they were obviously pretending. Envious, and overcompensating for my cynicism, I told myself there was no way their joy was real.

I didn't think it was possible.

6

THE GREAT MYTH

One sunny morning shortly after the COVID-19 superbug first swarmed the globe, during quarantine, my youngest daughter and I sat at the kitchen table listening to music and coloring. "The Rose" by Bette Midler came on and hit me. My soul awoke. Abuzz, my heart stood at full attention. I remembered my seventh-grade chorus recital. A troupe of students filled the risers in clean, white dress shirts and black pants. Blinding lights kept us from spotting our proud parents in the audience as our music teacher guided us through what was just another song at the time, but gut-wrenching as I listened in my kitchen that day.

I've always loved this song and now understood why it stayed with me for more than twenty-five years. Tears welled up as Bette sang my story, a story that is not mine alone. It's the story many of us suffer from internalizing: The Great Myth. The lyrics spoke to my unconscious belief: Love was painful and heartache was inevitable.

Happiness wasn't possible, and if I was lucky enough to glimpse a bit of joy, it wouldn't last. I was convinced love artfully doled out unscrupulous suffering while hiding under sweet gestures. Unable to offer myself wholly, I apathetically awaited the day when my partner would leave me or hurt me, and he undoubtedly would. Trusting no one, I spent my life protecting my fragile heart. The saddest part of all, I prided myself on thinking this was wise.

Listening in dismay, I crumbled as her words shot through to my heart. I wondered if this was a curse. Timely as they are, my spirit homies came to the rescue. They swept me up in their magical arms, comforted me, and gave me a safe place inside to get real. Most curses turn out to be blessings, and this was the best one yet.

But before the blessings could bestow upon me, I had to jump into the deep for a pummeling, no matter how torn up and bloodied I knew I would get.

I was under the waves, pulled out by the undertow into the uncharted territory of my soul. The waves thrashed me around and ripped my heart in two. Lonely and afraid, I lost faith I would be delivered to safety in one piece. The waters of uncertainty had to nearly drown me before I decided to relentlessly heal my broken spirit.

I accepted the mission to heal when I entered recovery. I was not hiding from reality and felt the painful events as deeply as I could but denied myself permission to be genuine with all my emotions. It appeared that I was dealing well with the blows of life, but fear prevented me from moving through the grief process completely—not just grief from death but grief from other loss. I couldn't face the magnitude of pain I was tasked with feeling in the various stages of my sobriety. I was going through motions, taking actions as my twelve-step program saw fit to stay sober—going to therapy, taking counsel from wise women, and praying—but never releasing control of my emotions long enough to allow the universe to bring unlimited health and wellness. Scratching the surface of each loss, I ventured into the pain briefly and ran away when it became too great. Resisting the hard work necessary to heal, I shut down a piece of my heart after each loss and sank further and further into darkness.

Unable to heal and powerless to change, I unconsciously protected my heart by overthinking every move and controlling my surroundings and actions. Scaring myself out of trusting and loving to the best of my ability, I kept just enough distance between you and me to feel safe. Denying myself the beauty of being all in with my feelings and with you, I lived in a hellish kind of purgatory. I sensed something was off but did not have the courage to dive deep enough and stay long enough to get honest with my pain.

I stayed there for more than a decade.

While listening to "The Rose," a conversation with Colleen from 2009 came into focus, as it had at other times but not with such clarity. She told me feelings of inadequacy kept me afraid of emotional intimacy, thereby holding me separate from relating to others on a deep and meaningful level. I was unwilling to show my vulnerable self for fear I wouldn't measure up to the ideal I had planted in my mind, and other people wouldn't measure up either. One of us would surely disappoint the other. (The work Colleen and I did at this time surrounded friendships; it did not translate to romantic relationships. That came later in my work with Tracy.)

I was more comfortable with a friend in a coffee shop than in her house. It was too close. Masquerading was drudgery in an intimate environment like someone's home; faking instigated discomfort. There was an emotional disconnect between who they were and who I was. It was as if I lived on a submarine sunken beneath gallons of anxiety, and they cruised along comfortably on a yacht, piña colada in hand. I could not match their level of vulnerability.

This disconnect unnerved me, and keeping busy, along with ingesting various substances, was the antidote for soothing those nerves. I was once told it was rude to continuously clean while I had guests. I thought I was helping to make things nice. I wasn't cleaning for my guests. I was keeping busy to avoid interaction. My need to be preoccupied outweighed my need to be *with* people for fear of being seen, unliked, and unaccepted. I had no idea who would even appear if I allowed myself to be seen. I had carefully curated a facade to overcompensate for my lack of self-worth.

Anxiety drove me into a heightened state of control well into sobriety. I noticed while hosting dinner parties I was compelled to keep the table free of dirty plates, the cloth napkins refolded and placed neatly at my guests' seats. I scraped crumbs so things appeared neat and under control. Under control meant good. It meant I was good. I had to be working, working, working, because if I wasn't producing by cleaning and topping off drinks, I held no value.

I spent too many evenings, holidays, and daughters' birthday parties cleaning and controlling, doing rather than being. My distress while in a state of vulnerability was paramount while sharing myself with friends, swapping stories, and engaging in fun. I could not relax and experience joy. I had flirted with this truth here and there, when feeling safe to do so, but I could not reach the heart of the matter.

I came close when I met Carole at two years sober. She was warm, all-accepting, welcoming, pure love energy. She let herself be seen, and I allowed her to see me. I showed her the bad, shameful little girl cowering inside my twenty-eight-year-old body. I trusted Carole to love all of me, and she inspired courage to love all of myself, but I was still uncomfortable in my skin and unable to share this with the world. I needed her to help me step into my authenticity, and it was only in her presence I felt safe to do so.

I felt the same way with my friends at the Pearl Jam concert as I did with Carole, and I could no longer accept bits and pieces of authenticity to show up at will. I needed to feel true to myself all the time, to find my self-love, and to take back my power. Or maybe I was seeking to feel my power for the first time.

Eleven years after that conversation with Colleen, I began to understand I was existing in a prison of my own making, self-protecting instead of loving myself and others. I was settling for a muted palette to color my days—living a half-hearted, insecure, and inauthentic life—instead of embracing the luminous hues of wholehearted living available to me. I could not unsee my truth as hard as I tried, and I became willing to change like never before. I had to be. If I ignored the glaring signs and the pain grew too great, I might have gotten drunk. And if I got drunk, I might die.

As you've read, this was not my initial reinvention. I've experienced willingness to jump into the future without skepticism before, offering up my heart to be filled with new, unfamiliar feelings. But it was the first time I was willing to risk emotional safety for love, to see who I would become when the boxing gloves came off.

I wanted to meet my authenticity. I needed to. My life depended on it.

I never fully subscribed to the good or the bad. Constantly wavering in between, in a state of indifference, I was either in the past or the future, sometimes both places at once. I wouldn't ground myself in today because today was too risky. The feelings that appeared in the moment might overwhelm, so I floated above and watched life happen, never truly taking part. I planned and prepared for another day while watching the one I was in slip away. Sure, there were good times, brief intervals when I was present and enjoying life, but if they lasted too long my anxiety built and I created chaos to ruin it.

Brené Brown, PhD, LMSW, is a researcher of vulnerability, shame, courage, and worthiness at the University of Houston Graduate College of Social Work. I read her book *Daring Greatly* in the midst of my darkness after moving to Colorado. Brown calls this type of emotional self-protection "foreboding joy."[2] It's the inability to feel joy due to fear of forthcoming pain. It means I do not allow myself to engage with an open heart of absolute love and connection because I believe disaster is on the horizon. I learned this in 2016 and was intrigued; this concept felt close to home. Allowing it to occupy space in the back of my mind, I left it there and looked no further. I didn't understand the implications of foreboding joy in my life and the pain it was creating. I wouldn't allow myself to understand because I could not envision a path forward to change.

"Foreboding joy" robs me of the now like a thief in the night, stealing my prized possessions of love, trust, and connection. Lost in the moment I'm supposed to be enjoying, fear deviously rips me out of the present and drops me off in a painful future without my assent. I become detached and pull myself away from the people I'm with. It is not only unfair to me, but it's an insensitive way to behave with others.

The distance I keep is preparation for the pain. I prepare for loss before loss is a potential outcome. I'm a Pain Prepper, and it's exactly what I was doing in my marriage but didn't know it.

My husband's 9/11-related post-traumatic stress disorder and physical illness, along with our twelve-year age gap, created challenges for us as a couple and as a family.

Jim's twenty-five-year career as a civil servant in New York City took a toll on his health: mentally, emotionally, and physically. The scenes he attended as a transit police officer, a twenty-year-old boy in blue fighting crime in the subway system in the late eighties, and the bodies he pulled from burning buildings as a firefighter left an indelible mark on his psyche. Jim has responded to gory car accidents, once observing a decapitated body. He has wrestled dangerous weapon-wielding perpetrators to the ground. He's answered cries from hysterical women in front of his firehouse in Bushwick, Brooklyn as they begged him to save their babies from a fire.

Then there is the most traumatic: the tragedy at the World Trade Center on September 11, 2001. Jim worked many sixteen-hour shifts at Ground Zero over the course of nine months, searching the rubble for body parts to be presented to inconsolable widows and widowers and to children who would never see their mother or father again. He sought rest in a nearby church, where he cleared his lungs of poisonous particles and collapsed in a wooden pew as the Prince of Peace watched over, reinvigorating him to continue the recovery operation upon awakening.

Jim is a hero.

Post-traumatic stress disorder does not wear the face of disease but is a disease, one that creates behavior that is hard to understand—so hard that Jim didn't understand it himself. I, too, couldn't wrap my head around why he acted the way he did, and I was afraid his behavior was affecting our children. His hypersensitivity to his surroundings and hypervigilance progressed to the point that I didn't enjoy going places with him—not on a date, not to the school talent show, and not to Home Depot. And I certainly did not like how careful my daughters had to be around him, to not upset daddy. The pit in my stomach upon hearing the garage door open signaling his arrival home yanked the good vibes from the room. The kids and I were having fun, music turned up, dancing or making art, and when the dog jerked from his slumber at hearing the door lift, the fun screeched to a halt. Easy living turned to stressful, anxious living.

PTSD is progressive if left untreated, and Jim's sickness grew with the birth of each child. There was more for him to worry about, more to protect. It wasn't until nine years into our relationship and two daughters later that he admitted he was suffering and sought the proper professional help to treat this stealthy mental and emotional illness. When he did, I was already disheartened. I didn't know how to support him, and frankly, I was angry I had to deal with it. He asked me to read books, to learn more, but I resisted. It was his problem to deal with, not mine. Pretty selfish, I know, but I felt I had been duped; this wasn't what I expected when we said our vows at the altar.

His medical condition also frustrated me. The common cold turned into a sinus infection and sometimes pneumonia within twenty-four hours, laying him up in bed for a week. This happened a few times a year. I felt abandoned when he was sick and was mad I was left to take care of the children and the house without help. That was an easy scapegoat for my anger; I was scared he was going to die. Our generational age gap sharpened the focus, and the tapes began to play in my mind. I was going to be alone with two children and a broken heart. Denying this monstrous fear growing inside, I toughened up a bit more after each illness and plugged along, pretending all was fine.

All was not fine. Aside from my frustration about his conditions, I hardly knew the man I married. He had changed so much.

Jim was not the same man I met on the shores of Long Beach in 2007, the happy-go-lucky Irishman who offered me the shirt off his back the first time we hung out. He wasn't the laid-back beach bum who introduced me to the liberating feeling of wind blowing through my hair while riding cruiser bikes on the boardwalk, inhaling the fresh air of the Atlantic Ocean. Gone was the man who introduced me to hidden gems in the city, the guy who held my hand as we strolled along the cobblestone streets of Soho after a delicious dinner. Later, we sipped espresso on the broken sidewalk outside his favorite cafe. We went to historic music venues, independent movie theatres, and renowned art exhibits. My biggest cheerleader, Jim encouraged me to go to graduate school to follow my passion for social work. He opened my world so wide, sparking life inside, and it was exciting. The world felt like my oyster, like our oyster. Together, we were two sober people who could do anything we dreamed of.

People change. That's to be expected, but my husband felt like a stranger to me, like night and day. I missed his liveliness, his jokes and good-natured attitude. The fun we had together was gone, the air sucked out of every space we both occupied. Once a solid match, the clashing of our energies grew over time. Our initial bliss gave way to hard reality; challenges arose, and I went inward. Our world got smaller and smaller. My fear of Jim dying from his chronic medical issues coupled with the progressive, constraining nature of his PTSD pushed us far away from each other. I fell deeper into The Great Myth. Our relationship was evidence that love hurts, and I began readying myself for severe pain. Jim was not the initiator of such feelings. He fit snugly into the erroneous belief system I had been manufacturing since childhood, the fear building up after each painfully mismanaged life event.

My mother told me years ago that once we admit a problem we have to deal with it, which is why I was choosing to deny it for so long. I didn't want to deal with it. There is a wide range of beliefs available to strengthen denial, and we gravitate to the ones that make us feel safe. The Great Myth was what I held onto to fortify my denial and continue living unhappily in my marriage, to accept my unhappiness. Although I did it unconsciously, it made sense to protect myself and keep my distance. I was deathly afraid of the loss that was coming. So, I resisted looking too closely at reality.

I heard a man say in a twelve-step meeting that pain is not what causes trouble; it's the resistance to pain that causes trouble. This Buddhist philosophy took on new life as I considered the pain of my marriage after the Pearl Jam concert. I understood that my resistance (desire to avoid pain) shows me what I need to open up to, because resistance indicates fear and most fear keeps me unwell. The greater the fear of facing pain, and the greater my resistance to step into it, the greater my denial.

At this juncture, I was dumbfounded. I knew my resistance meant I had to face my fear, but I had no clue how to bring the loving and generous man, who made me feel like a diamond in the rough, back into my sacred heart space. I wasn't sure I wanted him back in my sacred heart space.

I had a couple of options: I could be the martyr, wear my pain as a badge of honor, and complain to anyone who would listen about the bad hand I'd been dealt. Or I could step into the healing light—the light of love—and give myself permission to heal. Option two won out, and I joined my fellows on our walk of life, yet again.

Little did I know my world was about to go from black and white to technicolor.

7

THE RUPTURES

The day in the playroom when the rose garden turned from bright pink to black was the day I suffered my first mortal soul rupture. A piece of me took flight for a safe place as I stepped from that couch a shameful little girl. The next rupture happened two years later.

It's dark, except for the hint of late afternoon sun peeking through the shades. A heavy body is lying on top of me—heavy, because to a seven-year-old, a scrawny adolescent boy weighs about a ton. My neighbor pins me to his bed and begins kissing me. A tongue investigates the inside of my mouth as hands move around my body, over my clothes.

"Open your mouth. You know you like it. You know you like *me*," he cajoles. Knowing this is wrong—not only wrong, but bad—crossed with curiosity, left me confused. I didn't know if I liked what was happening or not. Either way, I was scared and addled. How did

I wind up on his bed? Did he read my mind to know I had a crush on him? Did that make this my fault?

My young, formative brain was unable to sort it out, but before I could find the answers it was over. A guardian angel broke through the door I was locked behind and rescued me. That's how I remember it. Reality, potentially blurred by a need to repress a greater trauma may be different. Exact events do not matter much. It was traumatic enough.

I've grappled with what to name this event. Molestation? Childhood experimentation? Sexual assault? To me, molestation seems more extreme than what happened. Given his age, this could not be considered childhood experimentation. Sexual assault is most accurate, but I've decided to place it under the broader label of sexual trauma. Regardless of what I call it, it affected me deeply. My first kiss was forced upon me. My body and soul were violated. I was bad again, dirty, and full of more shame. Another piece of my innocence took flight for safer quarters.

I do not blame my neighbor for what he did, or my babysitter for the trauma inflicted on me when I was five. I don't blame my parents for what happened. They left me with people they trusted. This is a soul lesson; my deepest pain brings me to my deepest healing. Now, I get to share that healing with you, giving you a safe place to heal alongside me.

That's the purpose of my suffering, the reason for my ruptures.

I was offended when I wasn't invited to a party I didn't want to go to. Read that again. Can you relate? I wanted to be invited whether

I liked the person doing the inviting or not. I needed that person to like me. I knew the unrequited desire for friendship was not healthy but didn't know how to stop wanting to be liked—or why I even wanted people to like me when I didn't like them. During twelve-step recovery work, as well as in marriage counseling, I learned how the fear of emotional abandonment drove this thought process.

Emotional abandonment sounds harsh, but it's not always as severe as it seems. It doesn't arrive only in the form of trauma, abuse, or neglect. The scales vary. Some experiences with emotional abandonment are highly traumatic while others are not as taxing, and the extent to which an individual's soul wants to grow determines how deeply a person is affected by these events.

They say children are resilient. When falling from a bunk bed and bouncing to their feet, sure, they're resilient. When it comes to emotional trauma, I'm not as sure. It takes little for some children, especially more sensitive ones, to experience trauma that will affect them their entire lives. Some do not bounce back as easily as when dropping five feet from the top bunk.

There's a reason some people are more sensitive than others. Those souls are here to experience a high degree of emotional evolution. Regardless of severity, or sensitivity to emotional abandonment, a need goes unmet and a piece of our soul recedes to a place inside, hidden away. Afterward, these pieces subconsciously and consistently yearn to come forward. Our needs fervidly beg to be met.

A piece of my wholeness disappeared the moment my sexual innocence was stolen when I was a child. A part of my soul retreated to protect my brain and my heart, leaving a deep feeling of distrust and loss in its wake. This pain was compounded years later.

My mom's mom, Grandma Tessie, died from pancreatic cancer when I was twelve. Her passing sucked the vitality out of our family tree. She held our lifeblood, and her death left us empty, drained. My mom and Jeremy took it the hardest; I don't believe either recovered. Seventh grade—that's when my family of origin began to collapse. It's when *I* began to collapse. It's the year I smoked my first cigarette, a Kent III stolen from my mother's leather-bound cigarette case. Hiding behind the aluminum shed in my yard, inhaling nicotine for the first time, I felt powerful and was off to the races.

Four years later, the summer of my sweet sixteen, our family situation worsened. Mom was diagnosed with breast cancer and underwent a mastectomy. Still grieving my grandmother's death and consumed with fear she might die from cancer, mom struggled to stay in tune with how Jeremy and I felt. Our physical needs were met: The fridge was stocked with food. I had three different-colored pairs of Converse sneakers. And she made sure our schoolwork was done, and done well. But she had no idea how to help us process our fear (or our grief from Grandma's death). Our emotional needs went unmet.

It wasn't for Mom's lack of trying to understand. Oh, she tried, begging us to go to family counseling, but we refused to take part. We went once, and Jeremy and I both stormed out in a huff, declaring we'd never go back. Incapable of expressing the pain inside our scared and confused teenage hearts, we didn't have the words and felt stupid in front of the therapist. Nor did we have the coping skills to deal with our pain, so we acted out with drugs and alcohol. Mom, at a loss for how to move through this excruciating time in her own life, was at a greater loss about how to address our growing addictions.

To add to the confusion, it was obvious our parents' marriage was failing. Hushed and heated conversations behind closed doors got our attention. Jeremy and I weren't privy to the mysterious whispers, but we knew something was brewing by the cheap shots Mom and Dad took at one another, followed by the silent treatment. Lone troops on the battlefield, we took advantage of our parents' distraction and partied harder.

Five years later, the mystery was solved. I called home from the State University at Albany, New York in the spring of junior year, and my dad's voice no longer boomed on the answering machine. Returning home for summer break, I traipsed into a dark living room where Jeremy was nursing a hangover. With a whole lot of gruff and a little bit of venom he said, "Guess who it is, Amanda." I named her immediately. Our get-togethers with a certain family had ended, and when Jeremy asked me to guess, it clicked into place.

When I was sixteen, the summer Mom was diagnosed with breast cancer, Dad had an affair with Mom's best friend since high school. The two were so close that my mother was her maid of honor, twice. Our families were so intimate that we called her "aunt" and her children "cousins." It was a short-lived, but intense, month-long affair; my dad and "aunt" rendezvoused almost nightly. This event was the defining moment in the crumbling of our family—more so, in the crumbling of my mother's trust. The two people who were supposed to be loyal to her had not been and had betrayed her with each other!

She found out about the affair and asked the two of them to sit down with her and come clean. They did. My "aunt" said she was in love with my dad. Mom didn't care who was in love with whom. She told them it needed to end and it needed to end now, and it did. My parents entered counseling and worked at it for a while, but their marriage was irreparable. The damage was done. My mother's heart was so shattered that a complete replacement could not make it beat with the rhythm of love again.

I turned twenty-one the summer I learned of the affair and Dad left, not for that woman but for another one. Jeremy and I both went off the rails as our disease picked up steam, beginning my spiral down into heavy drug and alcohol abuse. Any shred of trust I had in people who claimed to love me unraveled with speed, like the loose thread that knit our family together.

I felt abandoned physically and emotionally.

You need not experience this level of severity to feel emotionally abandoned, and it may occur not only from things done but also from things left undone: You lay in your crib, crying, attempting to soothe yourself for hours, and no one comes to comfort you. Or in preschool, when you were left with a stranger, arms outstretched, screaming for your mom or dad as they walked away, day after day, and your teacher was too busy to console you, or worse, she scolded you. Or when your father missed your dance recital because he was called into work, again.

Some of these situations are unpreventable during childhood, even natural, but we enter the territory of emotional abandonment when our emotions are consistently met with hostility or neglected altogether. Consistent negative responses (or lack of response) to normal, distressing life events create feelings of unworthiness, which lead to emotional abandonment.

Other people in our lives besides parents—teachers, coaches, extended family, or friends—can also make us feel this way, but to a lesser degree. It can happen unintentionally, such as when your drama teacher didn't support you after you lost the lead role in *Mary Poppins* or when you scored the three-pointer and your best friend was not in the stands to congratulate you. Or it can happen intentionally, like when you missed the winning goal that would have won your team the championship and the coach berated you in front of your teammates. These events do not produce the initial feelings of abandonment created by a caretaker but compound them.

On the other hand, your caretaker and other influential people in your life may have been loving but not enough for the reception to be grounded into your core. The nurturing may have been there but lacked consistency or did not feel genuine. It's also possible you remember it differently than it happened because you needed to learn a soul lesson. It doesn't need to be factual to be true for you. Neither accuracy nor severity equate to a particular emotional response or determine the level of healing required to move through pain. What matters is that you felt abandoned or rejected.

I minimized the events of my life whenever I had the chance unless I was intoxicated, when everyone within earshot heard my tale of woe. I wanted to be a good girl, and good girls sweep painful emotions aside in the name of gratitude. Perhaps it wouldn't hurt as much if I told myself someone else had it worse than me. Some of my experiences are incomparable to what others have gone through; this is true. It is also true that I should be grateful for my life, and I am. This attitude provides perspective, and although it's valid, my ache is my ache and yours is yours. My grievance is not any less significant than anyone else's, regardless of what created it, as no one can place a value on my pain but me. Negotiating my emotions by hiding them under gratitude did not make them go away. It made them come back with a vengeance.

The work of healing emotional abandonment and trauma involves accepting that you feel this way irrespective of severity. There is no need to minimize or justify our pain, and we certainly don't need to compare struggles to validate yours. It's your truth, and you get to decide what that truth is. It doesn't even matter whether it happened or was imagined—the pain exists.

It's real for you, and there's a reason for its presence.

8

TIME TO FACE
THE MUSIC

I needed to understand why my marriage was suffering, and this need was stronger than my fear of looking at what I might find. It was time to face the music, and myself. Rolling up my warm, grungy, flannel sleeves of security, I made some phone calls.

Confiding in a few women about my alarming feelings in Seattle, two of them advised me not to tell Jim. One said I needed to. That was Tracy. She warmly but firmly told me I needed to get honest if I intended to preserve the integrity of our relationship. If I didn't get honest, I would forever be living a lie. So, I told him about the attraction. I told my husband I didn't love him, and that I hadn't loved him all these years. Angry and shocked, he seemed just as confused about it as I was. A month later, both of us majorly confounded, riddled with anxiety, and in utter despair, we decided to get to the bottom of it. The strenuous effort put into our relationship for a good seven years prior left us depleted. Our desperation lit the dubious path to Tracy's office.

Divorce was on the table, but we were both willing to do the work and see where it would lead. My daughters depended on us to step up to the plate; we had to at least take a swing before breaking up the team. There was another child depending on us too—Jeremy's daughter. She and her mother moved to Colorado the same month we entered counseling, and I felt a duty to create a home of stability to welcome her into. Six months outside of her father's death, she needed her family to be present with as much balance and warmth as we could rally.

I both wanted to be in counseling and didn't want to be in counseling, but I went. With arms folded across my chest, legs crossed, I listened to Tracy explain the problem and was surprised to hear it wasn't entirely my fault, nor was it entirely my responsibility to fix. She explained what drove my dysfunctional thought pattern, the dark cloud I carried overhead that was raining on our parade: feelings of inadequacy and chronic self-sabotage. She dug into the issue underneath: low self-worth from receiving invalid shame-based messages that convinced me I do not deserve true happiness. This meant even if I was guaranteed bliss, I couldn't embrace it. Tracy told me I needed to look at this or I'd continue to find myself in the same storm regardless of who I was romantically involved with, perpetually wondering why. My brother's death intensified this dysfunction, thrusting me into a helpless state of self-destruction.

Defenseless against internalizing the shame-based messages, I heard them playing on repeat as I wept in front of Jeremy's casket.

Kneeling down next to me, they took my hand and told me to suffer because my brother had died. I grabbed hold of that deceitful hand and solidified the messages as my truth. Low self-worth and survivor's guilt had a stronghold on my self-perception, and it warped my thinking. How could I be thriving, knowing my brother never would? How could I arrive at his funeral with the measure of success I had while he was lying in a coffin? Why him and not me? My mind plotted a course to my own demise.

I was not thrilled about the work I knew was coming in therapy. It was big stuff. But I kept showing up to our appointments and kept listening, reticently. After four months, I went to both private and marriage counseling with reluctant curiosity, not sold it would work but intrigued by the process. Then I went because I wanted to be there, rounding the bases faithfully and purposefully.

Every bereavement was magnified after Jeremy died. Every pain felt incredibly raw, cataclysmic. Each loss was a fresh stab to the gut I could not douse with antiseptic and bandage up. Tracy sat with me as I felt the pain, cried, and talked. She listened and met me where I was with no desire to change my feelings. Her only mission was to guide me to healing, handing me bandages and showing me the gentlest way to apply them.

She taught me how to let people, places, and experiences flow in and out of my essence with ease, to be a "good griever," a concept I could not wrap my head around for some time. Before then, I held on to an idea, person, or place for security. I could not handle the perceived abandonment, no matter how big or small, imagined or real. I've always had a tough time with change and with letting go. She told me I do not have to rid myself of the loss if I choose not to. Rather, I can incorporate pieces of those people and places into my life, tucking them away in separate spaces of my heart. I do not have to fully let go of anyone or anything. Instead of furiously trying to remove the pain of those experiences, I blend it into my being and take it with me.

I started this process by creating a ritual for grieving my brother. Tapping into his spirit, I look for signs and listen for guidance on what to do or what not to do. Connection with Jeremy and the souls of my deceased family members, as well as my Master Guides and Higher Self, gives me direction and purpose. The painful losses feel nurturing to me now, no longer stabbing but soothing as I turn them into meaning.

In couples counseling, Tracy encouraged Jim and me to look honestly at both of our faulty belief systems. She was frank with Jim and said he needed to get serious about his healing work if I was going to. (As my mom likes to say, "It takes two to tango.") She told us we needed to seek wholeness each on our own, and then blend parts of our separate wholes to create a third whole together. Three separate entities: my whole, his whole, our whole, or as close to whole as we could get.

Even though Jim was willing to go to therapy, he was reluctant to dive into the deep end of his trauma. It was stalling our progress, and I was anxious to move our relationship forward.

One afternoon, sitting on Tracy's loveseat, I presented him with an ultimatum. He had to engage in intensive therapy to target his PTSD.

Talk therapy, a method he employed for years, wasn't cutting it. Tracy suggested EMDR (Eye Movement Desensitization and Reprocessing), a technique that uses light or another stimulus to move the eyes in a way that opens the limbic system part of the brain, the amygdala and hippocampus. This area is the storehouse of long-term memories and emotions. After these pathways are open, talk therapy occurs. During sleep, traumatic memories travel to the prefrontal cortex part of the brain where they are reprocessed. The hope is that the disturbance will no longer affect behavior as negatively as it once did.

Jim agreed to commence EMDR. We were now both committed to doing the work separately and together.

Years before we met, Jim attended a lecture on Imago Relationship Therapy, a marriage therapy based on Imago Theory. Throughout our relationship, he occasionally spoke with reverence about what he learned at that lecture.

In the *New York Times* best-selling book, *Getting the Love You Want*,[3] Dr. Harville Hendrix and Dr. Helen LaKelly Hunt, founders of Imago Relationship Theory, outline the process of attraction known as romantic love and the path to true love, the relationship stage following romantic love. They explain why butterflies in the early days of romance take flight and how compassion steps in to create a deeper, more secure attachment based on trust. This highly effective, logical form of therapy teaches couples to love the whole person, not just the parts that serve our needs, which is the main attraction upon meeting.

Imago Theory, the driving concept of Imago Relationship Therapy, suggests that years after the initial rupture of emotional security in childhood, we tirelessly seek partners to cure our feelings of abandonment. It suggests we unknowingly sense mixed traits of our caregivers in our partners—ones that serve us and ones that do not—in an attempt to heal our childhood wounds. Fractured by our parents' humanness or their own unhealed trauma (or perhaps at birth when divine connection was severed), we notice subtle traits in our partners we think will make us whole again. The possibility of someone filling our void brings euphoria. Those are the butterflies you feel.

Symbolic of this psychology is feeling as if another person completes you. Hendrix and LaKelly Hunt say this indicates you are with a person who resembles your caregivers, which begets the chance of getting what you always wanted and needed—the connection and aliveness you felt with your parents at birth. You are constantly searching for this sense of aliveness through your "imago" or image. Your partner is that image. Your imago, or reflection of your "lost self," is made up of the pieces of you that submerged deep within the moment you became aware your caretakers could not meet every childhood need. Taking a step further, I suggest we are constantly searching for pieces that submerged after trauma induced by people other than our parents. We are compelled to create alliances with people who bring our "lost self" to the surface so we can put our pieces back together. Hendrix and LaKelly Hunt suggest we do not know this is happening while falling in love.

The seven-year itch seems to be an accurate timeline for marriage testing. All is well for a while, then you realize the fantasy is not reality as your partner fails to meet your expectations. The dream comes crashing down like the demolition of a sacred altar—the altar of hope. The fairytale gives way to the drama, and the rubber meets the road. The dream crashes because the parts of your caretakers you needed and sought in your partner were never in your partner to begin with. What you saw were the parts your caretakers lacked, largely through no fault of their own; they too are products of their own experience and most likely did the best they could. This means we think we've found a partner who can make us whole, but actually we sought a partner to recreate emotional abandonment. We hoped our partners would change to meet our needs, even begged them to, but they didn't or couldn't because they weren't equipped to. They didn't know how to. Painful feelings of emotional abandonment resurface from our "old brain" (the limbic system), and we feel let down.

This is as it should be; it's not a bad thing. It's why we are drawn into partnership and serves our personal development and healing if given sufficient attention. If dealt with properly, the dynamic serves to bring us closer to whole, but not without some inner turmoil first.

Neural pathways were carved in our "old brain" during childhood when we experienced feelings of abandonment. Upon realizing our partners cannot deliver us to wholeness, we re-experience these painful wounds, and those neural pathways become stronger. Problems arise. Desperation flares. Frustration and anxiety present. Instead of understanding the origin of the problem, we tell ourselves we selected the wrong mate for a hundred other reasons. Convinced a different partner will make us happy, we are unaware our wounds need healing.

The goal is to create a safe space between you and your partner where new neural pathways become more well-worn than the pathways that screamed "Danger! Danger!" when needs went unmet. A safe space is built when you vulnerably identify wounds and communicate longings, trusting your partner is willing to change to meet your needs and vice versa. This challenges the common belief that you should not have to sacrifice any part of you to serve someone else—a person should love you exactly as you are, and ideally they should. However, if parts of your personality or learned behaviors inhibit you from being in a pure, loving partnership with another, then a change (with healthy boundaries in place) is certainly called for. (Note: Every suggestion in this book is void when abuse of any kind is present.)

In changing to meet your partner's needs, you rediscover the lost parts in yourself that created the void, bringing you closer to whole. Becoming who you were always meant to be, you fill your own needs and your partner's. Your partner fills his or her own needs and yours. Consistent, healthy behaviors create new, safe pathways resulting in a secure attachment to self and your partner.

Jim brought this philosophy to Tracy's attention as a possible cause for our problems. She knew much about it, said she was using Imago concepts in her technique with us, and suggested we look further into it on our own. We were willing to investigate the legitimacy of Imago Theory playing out in our relationship, and our COVID quarantine was the ideal time to explore.

Between bouts of wanting to run away when the vulnerability became too great, we forced ourselves to meet once a week to go through the Imago workbook. This was another strenuous effort we hoped would turn the key and unlock both of our battered and bruised hearts, which were not as bruised as when we started counseling but were still quite sore.

Mine was, at least.

9

BOUNDLESS
EXPANSION

Despite my feeling of apartness and perceived loss of self after moving to Colorado, I did not have to forfeit my identity as a New Yorker to feel a sense of belonging. I didn't need to extricate my core identity of street smarts, a direct approach to things, or my affinity for the ocean in exchange for line dancing, summer snow, and the majestic energy of a 14er. I did not have to abandon any of my attributes or affections.

Instead, I assimilated by embracing and incorporating new ways of living, by communicating differently but effectively. I respected and welcomed the cultural differences foreign from how I lived on the East Coast, making room for them without having to get rid of my New Yorkness. Breaking new ground without having to replace one culture with the other, I augmented my being to allow both to fit inside without feeling like I was betraying my truth. Expanding, I became richer in character and spirit.

Existing authentically in both places proved more than one truth can be true at the same time. It is true I love New York; I miss the people, the beach, and the city. It's also true I do not want to live there. I feel closer to my soul in Colorado, at least for now. As a multidimensional creature, I can have varied beliefs and feelings about the same event, situation, or place—or about me. One belief does not make the other moot, and they each hold a valid place on my spectrum of appreciation.

This brings me to a new way of living I call Boundless Expansion.

My Boundless Expansion was lingering for a long time, patiently waiting to be roused, not knowing how to step forward—present, yet elusive, like the word caught in your mind you can't put your finger on.

The inception took place in 2010 on our honeymoon at a Sandals resort on the island of Saint Lucia. A tropical storm set in on the second day of our trip. There isn't much for a sober couple to do on a rain-soaked island, and I was getting antsy. During a 10:00 a.m. game of *Name That Tune* in the lobby with drunk newlyweds, I turned to Jim and asked if we could go home. It was summer, and we lived on a white, sandy beach. Jim suggested we go elsewhere. I stared at him blindly. His proposal blew the lid off my limited view of possibility. My finite mind did not stretch far enough to digest the preposterous suggestion to go to a second location. Having no idea what flexibility felt like, I was stumped by his island-hopping proposition. Then the lightbulb went on, and I asked myself, *Why not?* We checked the storm's route, phoned our travel agent, and were seated on a flight to the Bahamas the next morning. This was Boundless Expansion in its infancy. I felt the shift inside, the broadening of my mind and heart, but couldn't imagine where I was headed with these thoughts and feelings.

Boundless Expansion, as its name suggests, is wildly larger in range and carries more depth than seeking out an alternative solution. It is the home of exponential, unending growth of mind, body, soul, and spirit housed within my heart space. It's the amplification of my emotional nature to such an extent that I make room for every thought, feeling, and attribute to comingle peacefully without having to reject any of them. The hole in my soul is filled with these pieces and is constantly widening to encircle the tender and bristly parts of myself, as well as the tender and bristly events that come to pass. I find a neat little place for each one to live with neither fear of intrusion nor judgment of their value.

It may sound complex but is the home of simplicity. When we're safe in each emotion, attribute, or event as they appear, lucidity arrives. Our innards become flexible, nimble like a gymnast, stretching far to welcome ourselves with total acceptance. The need to push away any emotion vanishes while our capacity to embrace emotion grows. The amount we stretch to welcome pain is directly proportionate to the extent to which we can welcome peace. Our hearts can house joy, despair, excitement, and worry, acknowledging each one whenever and however they arise. Whether our emotions are anticipated, back-to-back, or unexpected, we fluctuate between them calmly and confidently. We watch them roll in, then away, like clouds—both the dark and stormy ones and the fluffy, white ones.

In the summer of 2020, I started putting together pieces of the puzzle Tracy was laying out for me in counseling over the previous two years. Learning to be a "good griever" taught me how to accept the tidal wave of grief that could not be contained after Jeremy died. Feeling safe to embrace and release people, places, and events, I began to feel safe embracing and releasing parts of myself. The "good griever" concept shifted from an imaginary place outside to a habitat within. Anchored far down, it reached my core and cannot be expelled.

Tracy told me to visualize a classroom of little Amandas, each sitting at her own pint-sized desk. She helped me see the one little Amanda with her arm up, bouncing up and down in her seat begging, "Pick me! Pick me!" (Apt, because that really was me in fourth grade.) She told me that girl is my self-protection. She's the one who comes to my rescue when the dark clouds roll in and I become frightened that the fluffy, white ones will not return. She's the little girl who took flight during my sexual trauma, yet lingers close by to guard me when necessary—the one who dressed me in emotional armor after my father left to ensure my heart would never break like my mother's. She is my greatest defense mechanism.

Tracy said to kindly ask her to take a seat at the back of the class and sit tight, because I do not need her at the moment. There will be a day I will need to call on her, but today is not the day. It may be next Tuesday, next November, or in twenty years, but I will invite her up to the front again. My track record tells me she will be back.

After our session, I met that little girl and hugged her. Holding her on my lap, I told her she is loved but I cannot have her in the front of the class. She doesn't allow the rest of the children to have a voice when she is waving her hand in my face, trying to protect me from experiences I must grow from. It was hard. We cried. I assured little Amanda she was not abandoned, then took her by the hand and led her to her newly assigned seat.

Next, I invited little Amanda named Hope to come say hello. Once unwilling to enter into love, and living in fear, she was now hopeful she could heal. After Hope, Faith stepped forward and took the vacant seat her protector once occupied, front and center. Faith is the girl who knows, whether life throws her a perfect pitch or a curveball, she will be okay. She can trust herself or one of the other Amandas to surmount the obstacle.

I pictured the rest of my traits sitting at a bunch of desks in that classroom. Some of the girls had ants in their pants; others sat quietly. Some had untidy, messy hair; others had hair tamed in neat braids. Some girls knew the answers to the teacher's questions while others sat uninterested. Each Amanda had her place, and each unique girl was valued the same. They were all loved and cared for by the teacher, forty-year-old me.

One of those girls in the classroom sought a savior (or two, or three)—a man who could relieve her feelings of emotional abandonment and offer wholeness. Today, I am my own savior because I did my inner child work and continue to do the work.

One of the twelve-step programs I attend suggests an inner child meditation that takes place on a beach. Little Amanda and I walk along the shoreline, holding hands, smiling at one another. As we come upon people from my childhood who hurt me, the ones who threatened my safety and left me feeling unlovable, we do an about-face and walk in the other direction, away from them. I no longer need them to provide love and acceptance because I trust myself to meet those needs. There will always be more inner child healing work to do. There is no finish line to cross as more layers appear underneath the ones that become exposed, but I've made a great start.

Inviting every aspect of your being to sit in your classroom and acknowledging each one as worthy is a prerequisite to living in Boundless Expansion. You then allow these special parts to play together, respecting each other's flaws and attributes. Each part gets the same amount of love and attention as they all work in unison to create a secure, limitless identity.

Who is your savior? Who has your back when the dark clouds roll in? Is it your partner? Your parents? Your best friend? We need these people for support, but let them surround you and your Higher Power in the center. Be your own savior. Be the teacher in the classroom *and* the children. Encompass yourself as fully as possible so you feel safe and protected without needing someone to come to your rescue. The truth is, no one can do it for you so you must save yourself.

And we all need a little saving now and then.

10

ALL OF ME

I am my own worst enemy, my harshest critic. This character flaw serves me well at times. It keeps me in a constant state of competition with myself to evolve into a better Amanda. I wouldn't remove this or any other character flaw, because the pain they cause forces me to push beyond my fear and to heal. Getting honest about my flaws (or character traits that do not serve me well) and turning them into attributes (traits that do serve me well) are requirements for trusting myself.

Which parts of you create pain, yet you won't change? And why won't you change them? Fear not: Your character flaws, the parts that cause unhappiness, also serve you and others well when used correctly. Transforming a flaw into an attribute is called integration, a tool I picked up in recovery.

Before you can integrate, you must understand these character flaws serve you in the midst of the pain they cause, which is why you continue the behavior even if it's not good for you. Predictability of emotions makes us feel in control, so we choose to stay in the problem. If our flaws did not serve us in some way, even though we swear we hate them, we would stop letting them guide our actions immediately.

Your flaws are not your fault. Flawed character traits start out as natural, human instincts and become distorted as life has its way with you. Painful experiences force us to use our God-given traits in ways we are not proud of to protect ourselves, and in some cases, to survive. The secret is to change the handicap into a useful resource. Instead of serving you in a limited way, it now brings abundance. It takes an honest approach and creativity to integrate the parts that aren't working for you into ones that do.

My instinct for financial security made me stingy. The instinct to be accepted by others pushed me to fall in with the wrong crowd. My instinct for attention fashioned a loudmouth. But those instincts were given to me for a reason, so instead of anxiously trying to remove these parts, I use them to serve me and those around me. My instinct for financial security makes me a good money manager. My instinct for acceptance makes me treat others the way I want to be treated. My instinct for attention makes me smile at random people on the street, initiating a good feeling for both of us.

Let's look at another trait I am positive is not mine alone: the perfectionist, the consummate overachiever. I create unreachable expectations for myself, setting a goal and almost reaching it before moving the bar higher. This keeps me in an endless state of striving. I rarely allow myself the satisfaction that comes with achievement, limiting my self-actualization.

Perfectionism also does not serve me so well in relationships. The high standards I set for myself project onto others. It leaves them feeling judged and not good enough. No one wants to feel like he or she can't live up to another's standards. That's the downside. The upside is I am determined and structured. Perfectionism pushes me to be proactive and to achieve success. It brought my family through the thick of the COVID-19 pandemic safely. I set high behavioral standards and disciplined myself to live by those standards for more than a year.

I'm a military operation kind of person, and it can hurt me or help me. It hurts when it presents as pressure placed on myself and others. It helps when it shows up as unrelenting perseverance. This pressure brings another trait to the forefront: compulsivity.

My compulsive nature helps me to not procrastinate, to be productive, and to accomplish tasks with efficiency. It hurts me when I feel forced to act quickly or make hasty decisions that backfire and cause difficulty for me and others.

Hypervigilance also has the potential to both hurt me and help me. My survival instincts, as well as my constant search for my missing pieces, used to manifest as hypervigilance. I thought I was observant, a good judge of character. I now know I focused on the behaviors of people, places, and things to ensure my existence. On high alert, hypertuned in to the world around me, I was in a constant state of noticing and judging gestures to determine if I was safe (emotionally and physically) and accepted.

Once misinterpreted as observance, my vigilance is now an instrument for conscious interaction, helping me go deep into an inexorable, safe connection with everything around me. No longer scanning my surroundings for directions on how to act, browsing gestures for information about who you want me to be, I am aware of opportunities to sincerely join my fellow humans in pain and in joy. Instead of worrying about my safety and acceptance, I'm free to think about how to meet and love you.

One more example: the elephant-addresser—the teenage girl with a big mouth who said what she thought needed to be said. The motive for "telling it like it is" was to get attention. It didn't matter if the attention was positive or negative as long as all eyes were on me. I've learned it's not what I say but how I say it that makes the difference. Today, I relay truths lovingly and kindly so others can hear me. The speaking is not as important as the reception. This is a skill I've honed over the years, one that means life or death in the recovery work I do. Through this inner work, I have transmuted the loudmouth, untrustworthy young adult into a closed-mouth, reliable confidante who can say what needs to be said without being harsh, most of the time.

I capitalize on painful traits by turning them into tools for connection, and this connection comes to life through awareness and acceptance of every character flaw and attribute inside me. I must meet my own parts first if I want to meet you in yours. When I see me, I see you, and when you see you, you see me, and when we see each other we connect. When your whole self is witnessed, internalized, and healed, you will see goodness inside you, then goodness all around.

Awakened by glory, you may feel compelled to connect compassionately, lovingly, and with trust.

Healing my fear of emotional abandonment taught me how to nurture more emotions and attributes than I knew I had. I learned how to love all of me, but I had to be mangled pretty badly first.

Pain pushed me to go through the process of observing, reflecting on, and accepting the parts I did not appreciate because I viewed them as bad. My parts weren't bad. They needed healing. Loving all of me, I am able to be present with my feelings without judgment. Without judgment, I need not reject any part because I do not view that part as unworthy. Accepting all of me, especially the parts that need healing, brings a deep sense of emotional security, the opposite of emotional abandonment.

Emotional security is the ultimate freedom, the stabilizing root of my soul. It grants me courage to feel it all: pain, passion, love, and loss. Accepting, loving, and honoring all my character flaws, attributes, and emotions helps me trust I will show up for myself, as myself, no matter who stays or leaves. Confident in my ability to handle the changing seasons of life, I'm free to be all in. The voices (past, present, external, or within) that attempt to lead me away from my True Self have quieted down. Neither outside forces nor my own inner critic hold the power. My devoted spirit now holds the power. In this space, I am safe to connect with love and let go in peace.

When I choose the path of insecurity, as I sometimes do, I get back on the horse and honor myself again, continuing to alter character flaws while embracing and accepting those flaws as part of me. I celebrate the source of who I am while keeping an eye out for the parts that need healing.

By acknowledging, welcoming, and healing the characteristics that create self-judgment, I take steps toward emotional security.

Harness self-acceptance and self-love to transmute your character flaws into a field of beauty that works for you. Mix all you are—faith, hope, joy, insecurity, doubt, fear—together to serve you, such as flowers mixing with weeds in a meadow.

During our COVID quarantine, my husband and I divvied up "off duty" days from our children. Taking advantage of my sanity breaks, I researched an adventure for a solo trip every Friday and found a magical place: Butler Gulch Trail near Winter Park, Colorado. It's a five-mile, moderately difficult hike over creeks, through towering pines, past waterfalls and meadows of flowers, culminating in gorgeous vistas above tree line. It was early July, and the wildflowers were at their exquisite peak.

About two miles in, I noticed an open space adjacent to the trail. The sun seemed to shine extra brilliantly on a patch of grass surrounded by tall trees. I had to enter it. Veering off the path, I sat in the middle of the patch. The birds sang their songs as I became one with nature, and I decided to lie down closer to Mother Earth. Water rushed in the nearby gulch, and clouds leisurely sauntered by as I witnessed God's splendor bursting at the seams. I began to notice the beautiful flora around me: purple columbine, yellow sunflowers, and white daisies. I noticed the weeds too: sprawling dandelions, spiky thistle, and encroaching crabgrass. A large flower resembling a rose caught my attention.

The song "The Rose" and my experience with it in my kitchen a couple of months earlier came to me. Moved by something other than myself, I stood and walked gingerly over to the flower. Taking a knee, I cupped it in my hands as a tear streamed down my cheek. I could feel my broken spirit deep within, and it was healing. Starting to weep, I saw little Amanda, felt her pain, and told her she was okay; I was near and would never leave her. God was near and would never leave her. I explained that no matter what painful experiences she had been through and will continue to go through, her spirit will never lose its vibrancy. No matter who or what attempts to dim her light, it will never cease shining.

I accepted myself for who I am, a product of my experience, and forgave myself for allowing The Great Myth to deceptively infiltrate my life and the lives of those I love. Hidden, as it were, for all those years, my spirit shone again in that meadow. I found it in that wildflower, nestled among the weeds of protection. The black roses outside the playroom window turned bright pink again.

I considered pulling the flower from the bush to take it home and dry it, but I didn't. It belonged there, in that field, with God's splendor smiling upon it.

It was safe.

11

A HUMBLE ADMISSION

The meditation cave is where it all goes down. It's the spiritual vortex in my home where I commune with my Higher Power and Higher Self, the sacred space where I seek guidance to treat the rifts in my soul. I become honest about who I am, exploring the qualities that serve me and those that do not. The cave is where I'm given courage to look squarely at the experiences that shaped me. It's where the heavy lifting happens.

This room and the articles in it help me get in the zone, trance-like. It's an eight-foot-by-eight-foot walk-in closet adorned with candles, inspirational signs, a two-hundred-year-old teak wood carving from Thailand, healing stones, and spiritual literature, all which create a discernable, high-frequency energy. This energy grants me humility to admit I do not have all the answers. Graced with willingness to experience a shift in consciousness, I become in tune with myself and the collective on a vast emotional level.

I don't walk into this room with humility or willingness. I take actions to open myself up to receive these gifts, ones that help me consciously gain access to God's love and light. I heal my energy, the fear and wounds blocking my connection to source energy, and then I attempt to heal the world's fear and wounds by sending love and light out to creation.

I do not leave this experience in the cave. When I've taken these steps in earnest, I step out recharged and ready to love. Taking my connection to a Higher Power with me wherever I go, like a little friend in my pocket, I am in constant communication with this energy. If I keep my eyes, ears, and heart open, it guides my steps. This energy is my North Star; I trust the direction in which it leads is good.

You do not need an angelic place filled with hallowed items to commune with whatever source you believe is helping you: Christ, Buddha, Gaia, Allah, Helper Spirits or Master Guides. The requirements are that you understand this higher force is not you, you establish a personal relationship with it, and you trust it. Do you trust in a greater force to guide you as you move through your days, making hundreds of choices that affect your life and the lives of those around you?

Let me clarify. The higher force, being inside you, is you and is also not you; the two are intrinsically intertwined. I call it Big G and Little G—G standing for God. Big G is the big man upstairs, and Little G is me. (My New York therapist Colleen introduced this concept to me.) Big G exists in Little G. However, Big G maintains its position as a force greater than you. Big G is the director and coproducer. You are the other coproducer. It's a partnership where one has more power, and both are mutually respected.

I ask my director to come into my heart, mind, body, soul, and spirit every morning, to show me the truth of what's going on in my life and to do for me what I cannot do for myself. Some mornings it comes quickly; other days I wait longer to feel it, but it always comes. Then, I pull out my journal and write. Sorting through both my fears and the guidance that's been graciously given, I peel layers to uncover the truth of whatever is bothering me. Trusting my Higher Power to expose my truth is the bedrock of trusting myself. When I trust Big G to guide me, I trust myself because Big G exists in Little G. We are one and the same.

I trust myself, yet check the guidance from both Gs with wise people around me to ensure that what I receive is coming from the spirit world, not just from me. Considering all the information presented, I incorporate the elements that feel right with a pragmatic yet soulful approach.

Times of uncertainty provide rich opportunity to become comfortable while uncomfortable, peaceful while searching for answers in distressing situations. This intimate space of commotion, the space of "not-knowing," another Buddhist philosophy, is where we exercise humility and willingness; it's where we admit we don't have the answers. It's also a great place to practice open-mindedness and patience.

Over time, sitting in the space of "not-knowing" without an answer and with an open mind leads to an accurate truth we can trust. Tracy's couch was the perfect place for Jim and me to do this.

I came back from Seattle with the conviction our marriage was inherently flawed, that the companionship I desperately sought was not possible. However, years in recovery taught me to dig and to question my feelings and emotions regardless of how strongly I felt them. It was highly probable something was going on under the surface, something my subjective eyes could not see. Jim's experience in recovery also taught him to look at himself and honestly consider if he played a part in our disconnection. We were both willing to "not-know" what drove our discomfort and enter therapy with an open mind. We were also willing to stay as long as we needed to, until our fear settled down and the truth became clear.

"Not-knowing" for months on end brought Jim and me to knowing. The humble admission that we had no idea what the problem was, never mind the solution, was the action that guided us toward meaningful communication and compassionate understanding.

Take the chaos and place it in the light of "not-knowing." Admit you don't have all the answers, that someone else might. View it as a chance to activate your open mind. Ask your Higher Power to rid you of willful answers so you can find honest solutions. Open up. Get curious. The gates will open, and thoughts will begin to drop into your consciousness effortlessly. Possibilities will emerge. Repeating this process brings more thoughts and more possibilities until you reach a solution based in love, a solution you can trust.

Keep your humanness green, and your willingness to learn greener. Your mind will continue to tell you that you have the answers; that's the human part. Tell your mind to settle down—the true answers are on the way. The more we live and see and grow, the less we know.

We are closest to our True Self when we know nothing.

I never had a hobby, no pastime to hang my identity on. Betsy played baseball. Annie was an artist. Richie, a runner. Me, nothing. Before getting sober, all I could say was "I am a Pearl Jam superfan, and a deep thinker—the philosophizer. Oh, and I could drink you under the table." But that was about it.

Activities were presented and encouraged by my parents throughout childhood and adolescence. I tried a lot, but nothing stuck—not soccer, not baton twirling, not lacrosse. I played a screechy violin for a few years in elementary school. Dance was a constant from preschool to sixth grade, the one activity to which I was committed for any length of time. I attempted much but could not claim any avocation as my own. I always quit. It wasn't because I was not good at these things. I was, but I was not good enough per my own standards. I believed I was not as talented as Betsy, Annie, or Richie and was in constant competition with my peers and myself.

Third chair in the orchestra or cocaptain of the JV cheerleading team when my friends were on varsity was not acceptable. I was either going to be the best or nothing at all. There was never a suitable in-between. Lacking humility, I found my place either above or below you. I was more comfortable above you because I was terrified of the devastating blow that accompanied defeat. (There's that pesky loss again!) Defeat meant I was unlovable. My perfectionism and my need to be accepted demanded me to be the cream of the crop. If I wasn't, I was a total loser, unworthy of the Carvel ice cream after the game. I took the bat I swung at the softball game my team had lost by a landslide and beat myself up with it. (Not literally.) I was jealous of the winners, then overcome with guilt for feeling jealous. I wanted to feel achievement for myself whether I won or lost and to be happy for others, but I didn't know how to get there.

An unwieldy road map was laid out in front of me. Instead of learning the street names and the turns to take, I frustratingly refolded it into a crumpled mess because I could not comprehend the directions offered. And the interesting part is if I tried, I excelled. But the voice in my head, the little liar, told me I would never succeed, so why try?

Once it became obvious I was not going to be the captain of the lacrosse team or the first chair violinist, I turned to what I was good at—drinking. When I put down the booze, I began the journey to discovering the real me and started coming into my own. I learned my favorite colors and my favorite foods. I became a runner and a reader. As the years progressed, I became a gardener, a baker, a licensed master social worker, a wife, a mother, a transplanted Coloradan, a seeker of all things spiritual. I am now a climate activist, a horseback rider, a drummer, a dancer (I leave it all on the kitchen floor), and a singer, whenever I get the urge to belt out a tune.

It doesn't matter if I publish a bestseller, paint a gripping master-piece, or run a marathon under four hours or at all—I am a writer, a painter, and a runner. I am what I say I am regardless of society's measuring stick of success. My identity is of my own making, and my success is based on how well I meet my own standards, not the demands of outside pressure. My worth is decided my me and me alone.

This takes a humble attitude to achieve. Accepting my abilities, skills, and aptitudes exactly as they are means I acknowledge my intrinsic talents as well as my lack. I'm not going to be good at everything. I'm not supposed to be, and that's okay. I am meant to nurture and grow my natural gifts as a unique offering to the world.

Today, I put away the rigid bat manufactured from self-judgment and low self-worth and take out the flexible feather of humility. I accept myself just as I am.

I am always worthy, lovable me.

12

EMOTIONAL
INTEGRITY

E motional integrity, by its nature, is personal. It is your innermost moral compass directed toward your heart, an unwill-
ingness to sacrifice your commitment to love and compassion
regardless of the situation.

You can present yourself to the world in a way that looks like
you have emotional integrity, but only you know if you embody this
characteristic. You must get honest with yourself about it if you want
to trust yourself. The path to honest emotional integrity is paved with
honest, integrous actions.

When I was three months into writing this book, my mother
was diagnosed with Non-Hodgkin's lymphoma. I decided to fly to
New York for her first chemotherapy treatment. Going back to my
old stomping grounds after writing many of these words was an

opportunity to see if I was living with emotional integrity, to show myself what I'm made of.

The rubber met the road when the soles of my high-top sneakers hit the pavement at LaGuardia Airport. After a year in pandemic solitude, I was now put to the test in the concrete jungle. Can I practice what I preach under all conditions? Will the tornado of temptation suck me in, causing me to default to past patterns and behaviors for the sake of emotional and physical survival?

New York is a rough place. If you've been there, you know. Some people describe New York anxiety, a frenetic energy that never quits—one I found hard to manage after six years of living a quieter life in the suburbs of Denver. Resensitized to the noise, honking horns, and fast pace, I was highly attuned to the vigilance one must possess to maintain safety. In high-alert mode, my pulse quickened.

I escorted Mom to chemotherapy on a rainy Monday morning. We had nine hours of excellent bonding time as the bags of poison slowly dripped into her veins. We ate decent hospital food, talked, laughed, and rested. Despite the relatively pleasant experience at the hospital, I arrived in New York with a sullen energy. I've taken a dozen or so trips to New York since living in Colorado. Many were not for pleasure; about half of my flights led to a funeral. This was yet another woeful trip for me.

The stress of flying unvaccinated in early 2021 as well as Mom's cancer diagnosis weighed heavily on me, and I was aware of my power to manifest a miserable week. Keeping this awareness with me like a crucifix pendant over my heart, I tried to be kind to all, as the Almighty would. Like I said, New York is a rugged place under normal conditions, so given my current stress level, I was going to have to work even harder to be gracious. It was a litmus test of my spiritual growth, my emotional integrity, and my boundary setting. And I wasn't doing too hot.

Self-care was a must. On Tuesday, I bolted to the Long Beach boardwalk for a run in my favorite spot in New York. Aside from my life there with Jim, I grew up nearby and spent many summers sunbathing with friends on that beach. The boardwalk is where I'd go to clear my head when life got to be too much; the ocean was my safe harbor as seagulls soared overhead, carrying my worries away. It feels like a separate universe to me. I'm sentimental about Long Beach and always will be.

Nature is the elixir of connection; the salt air and sea does wonders for a person's mood and is a great escape from the stress of Long Island. Determined to shift my gloomy disposition, I sought connection with the people on the boardwalk. After initiating eye contact, I flashed a big, friendly smile. They all smiled back. The positive connection to nature and to other humans did the trick. It raised my spirits.

As the week went on, a serious stressor concerning the health of another family member presented, and emotions ran high. I was hardly sleeping due to loud traffic outside my mother's apartment and the tenants upstairs, who seemed to be doing gymnastics all night. I do not do well on little sleep. To say the week felt like a constant assault on my patience is on point.

After five days of silently repeating the Serenity Prayer, I found myself back at LaGuardia Airport in the security line, looking forward to boarding my flight to Denver. My hopes were dashed when a Transportation Security Administration employee told me my ID would not scan and I needed to step aside to wait for the supervisor. I alerted him my flight was going to begin boarding soon and I did not have time.

My anxiety and frustration grew with each passing minute. After ten minutes, I stuck my face under the plexiglass divider, panicked I might not make it back to my sanctuary among the trees, and muttered a hostile sentence begging him to fix the problem. There was a short time when I was playing out a scene in my mind that would no doubt get me arrested. I was losing my cool, and I didn't care; my New York came out full tilt.

I started to wonder if this was a prank. Were my friends and family planning a wild surprise to honor me for flying across the country to take care of my mother? Was Eddie Vedder, Pearl Jam's heartfelt frontman and my favorite celebrity, going to mosey out from behind the X-ray machines and serenade me? (This is where my unchecked ego takes me!) As time went on, my mad went to scared and then to sad. I had to blink back tears. Despair forced me to turn to what works—the Holy Spirit, or as I like to call this omnipotent power, J. C. (Jesus Christ: my homeboy who always comes through in a clutch.)

I asked the Eternal Light to calm me down and show me the way. I was reminded to check my ticket and realized I had more time, but the clock was ticking. I started to breathe and walked my emotions back to the heart. My years of self-reflection taught me fear is the emotion under anger, so I tried to identify the fear, and it worked. I was afraid I'd never make it back to my peaceful abode. I started to put the situation in perspective, think positively, and believe the TSA staff would help me. I visualized myself walking through security and boarding the flight. I thought of my writing. I remembered telling you living with emotional integrity is one of my top principles. I would not be a fraud, and if I was going to publish these words, I had to live them.

After forty-five minutes, a supervisor arrived to tell me my ID still would not scan and I had to go to the end of the line. The end of the line! Would my ID magically scan after another half hour waiting behind hundreds of people? Peering at him above my double mask with desperation in my misty eyes I politely appealed, "I cannot do that, sir. I will miss my flight." He fiddled around for a few more minutes, stroked a few keys on the keyboard, and let me through.

I don't think my ID ever scanned. I don't know if the powers that be conspired to make the TSA supervisor let me go or if humility changed my demeanor and the vulnerable action that followed led me through security. Perhaps calming down inspired positive thinking and raised the frequency of my energy so the supervisor felt it and met me with compassion. Maybe it was all the above.

My mother says you catch more flies with honey than you do with vinegar. This particular fly had a two-hundred-foot wingspan and was headed eighteen hundred miles west.

I had four hours to examine my feelings over the previous week and my response to this most recent cortisol-spiking event. I realized I will always have work to do, but I've made progress. I am living with emotional integrity.

There were times during that week when I found myself alone, crying, clutching the pillow made from Jeremy's New York Giants jacket—times when I was lost between the old Amanda and the new Amanda, struggling to maintain my personal growth and shine my light. There were times of darkness, deep darkness. Again, I turned to my Higher Power. I got quiet, asked for guidance, and was directed to meditate and to listen. I heard a conglomerate of ideas, the most notable echoing a conversation with a friend earlier that week about suffering.

I heard this:

Be not afraid of your greatness. You do not have to go back into smallness when thrust into old realities. You can't go back. You are not that person anymore. You now have the ability to come out of suffering and into the light more quickly than before. Pain is necessary for your growth, but how long you stay in it is optional. You don't have to torture yourself in suffering for one minute more than it takes for the lesson to be learned. Do not squander the time you have on Earth when you can be doing the work of the heavens. Heaven is right here on Earth if you allow it to be.

The internal struggle is between fear and love, between darkness and light. That meditation reminded me the light will never cease its staunch attempt to declare victory. It is the most enduring facet of life. Darkness may win some of my battles, but my light will win the war.

That's what love does. It wins.

As I pondered the events of the preceding week, I felt happy to be heading back to the mountains. I also felt guilty for moving to Colorado, leaving my cancer-ridden mother in New York. Guilt creeps in when I think about how I'm not physically there for my friends and family when they need me. Logically, I know moving was the right decision and I don't regret it, but I often query the results of that decision.

It was during this stream of consciousness that I looked across the aisle and noticed a woman reading a book I had recently finished. The chapter she was reading was about self-care and putting yourself first. This was another moment of reassurance that the healthiest life I can live is one that prioritizes my well-being, a life of emotional integrity. It is also a reminder of why I need other humans. We end up in certain places at certain times as messengers. The woman reading her book across the aisle was my messenger that day. I need constant reminding of what's good for me and to not feel guilty about taking steps toward wellness. Thankfully, the reminders come exactly when I need them.

Preparing for landing, I put on a Led Zeppelin song that feels like home to me, a beautiful, melodic guitar instrumental. The wisdom of Confucius, "Wherever you go, go with all your heart," had been rolling around my brain for a few weeks prior, and it visibly showed up as we touched down. I looked at the ceiling of the aircraft and saw a heart made of light among the shadows. I came to realize home is not a place; it's wherever my heart is and can be in more than one place at a time.

My heart is my true home; its walls hold the hearts of the ones I love wherever I am on Earth. My true home isn't destination- or people-dependent. It's not found in my grandmother's candy dish in her Queens apartment or in the rainbow border that lined my childhood bedroom. People and places provide comfort and have their purpose, but my true home lives with source energy—compassion and love. Since source energy is all around me and inside me, I am source and my home is wherever I am. The only requirement is energetic, trustworthy connection to self, others, and the universe.

In this knowing, I'm safe in my being.

As these thoughts were forming, I recalled the sprout of this belief: One particularly distressing afternoon during my sophomore year of college, I attempted to quit school. After a long night of drinking and taking drugs that do not mix well together, I believed I was going crazy. Sneaking into my friend's dorm room desperate for a drink to calm down, I pulled a bottle of vodka from her mini fridge and took a nice, long swig. Trudging back to my room, I got into bed and drew the covers up to my chin to escape paranoia. Hallucinations flashed across my ceiling, and delusions filled my head as I lay there losing my mind until I couldn't take it anymore. Returning back to my friend's suite, I told her I was going to drive three hours south from upstate New York to Long Island. I wanted to cuddle with my dog on my parents' couch in their living room. I wanted to go home. I also told her I was dropping out of school and canceling the check in the mail for our upcoming spring break trip to Cancun. I did not trust myself to go on vacation; I might die in the land of free-flowing tequila and rum punch. I needed to go downstate and seek help.

She emphatically told me, "No way, Amanda. First, you cannot drive drunk. Second, if you can't stop drinking here, you can't stop drinking anywhere. You have to stay in school, and you have to get help." My friend, wise beyond her years, was right. So I stayed. I didn't get help because I wasn't ready, but I was forced to find safety in a place that felt dangerous to me. It wasn't the place that was dangerous; it was me. Looking back, I realize it was the first time I rooted into myself for protection. The feeling didn't last and I continued to drink, but the seed of safety was planted on my friend's futon that afternoon as I sat shaking and crying. I sensed a connection to my integrity and to the powerful source energy living inside me, a measly connection to my true home. It took six more years for this feeling to explode with vigor, but it did.

Breathing a sigh of relief upon arriving in the Front Range of the Rocky Mountains, I walked through the parking garage with a pep in my step, grateful and excited to see my family after a stressful trip. Welcomed by my dead Honda Pilot, I laughed out loud knowing it would work out fine. As long as I live with emotional integrity found deep within, I am safe.

I am home.

13

THE ASCENT

A friend (thank God for honest friends) told me I am addicted to chaos. She is correct. Serenity feels unsteady to me. Peace is something I do not trust will last. So, instead of being the victim of turmoil, I make it. I complicate issues where there are no issues to complicate. Do you do this too? I have a sneaking suspicion you might.

Why do we do this? First, because chaos turns on the chemicals, making us feel something, and we like to feel. It reminds us we are alive. Second, because it assembles a barricade between us and others, and we feel safe in apartness. We may not enjoy the chaos, but it's preferable to the risk of loss that comes with broken connection. It's safer than vulnerability.

Years after my friend's surveillance of my character, I learned why I could not surrender to serenity, why I nitpicked and drove a wedge between my husband and myself whenever I could. I did it to protect myself if the size thirteen shoe drops. Reality check: the shoe is most likely going to drop. That's life, for most of us. It's only a matter of when and what the dropping of the shoe looks like for you. When the steel-toed Dr. Marten boot dropped at the Pearl Jam concert, I had to decide if I was going to continue living in fear of vulnerability or find the bravery to love the best I can knowing pain is on the way. Luckily, my Spirit Guides made the decision for me.

Nine months into marriage counseling, in May 2019, our family took a trip to Crestone, in southern Colorado. We rented a house at the base of the Sangre de Cristo Mountains. I did not know until after the trip that Crestone is a spiritual vortex, and I didn't need Google to tell me. The energy mounted each foot we drove closer, and it was making me uncomfortable. I still felt disconnected to Jim at this time but felt a shift was coming—a shift I didn't know if I was ready for or even wanted. My heels of resistance dug into the mountainous desert, quicksand tugging me further and further down with each fear-based thought. I worried I would never emerge from the fear, that I would never change, that I wasn't capable of changing.

As we inched ahead over dirt and red rock rubble, we pulled up to the most ornate home I've ever been in. Adorned in a New-Mexico-meets-Morocco-meets-the-Far-East motif, there were no straight lines, only curves, and I loved it. More than décor, this space was richly appointed with spirit. It speaks to souls, and it whispered to mine, "Come in and relax." I put on the new age music found in the kitchen, and my girls and I danced on the bohemian runners, moving gracefully and easily. Our limbs uninhibited, we danced almost interpretively, and something happened. My rhythm was restored. I was rendered unable to hold back pure love for my children, my husband, and our family. The team was reuniting.

At last, I was willing to be all in, cards on the table, and I took another leap of faith.

I woke on the second morning and stepped outside to watch the sun rise over the snowcapped mountains. The scene I was eyeing should have been named "A New Day," not just because it was the start of another day, but because I felt the shards of my marriage mending into something new, something better—a new beginning. I conceded to the idea that broken does not mean over and knew we would be better for having been shattered. *I* was better for having been shattered. I opened my heart and readied myself to receive unconditional love, not only from Jim, but from divinity and from myself. I chose to activate eternal connection. I *chose*. That doesn't mean I entered into eternal connection. That happened during my COVID seclusion.

I have a healthy fear of dying with regret, and I refuse to die knowing I willingly gave up the life of love and healing my soul craves. As the day-breaking sun began peeking over the mountains, shimmering its radiant light on the treetops below, I promised myself I would learn to love to the best of my ability all the days of my life, in the sun and in the rain. The Blood of Christ mountains blessed me with a new life that morning. I came back from the netherworld I had been suspended in to rejoin the living, or maybe I blended the two.

I took a photo of the spectacle unfolding before me, healing me from the inside out. I printed it on canvas and gave it to Jim for our nine-year wedding anniversary that June. Nature is all around us in its beautifully whole and fractured forms, harkening us to behold the lessons and the principles it teaches. The answers we seek are in front of and within us if we take a hard look. "A New Day" lives in my meditation cave as a reminder that I can restart my day, my attitude, my relationships, and my life at any time.

I did not rise into willingness alone; neither does the sun rise over the mountains. Other forces of nature cooperate in the atmosphere to keep things in check, as do our souls to assist our greatest good. My willingness to ascend happened with the support and guidance of my village: loyal friends, seasoned professionals, a patient husband, and an all-loving Higher Power.

I turned to my recovery community, my friends who feel like family, and asked them to teach me how to love regardless of fear that bubbles up when I consider the loss that is coming. I asked them to show me how to heal. Watching them move through life's greatest challenges with tenacity motivated and guided me as I began my journey to feel safe to love and let go. They gave me hope when I was hopeless and believed in me more than I believed in myself.

Entering into partnership with loving souls, nature, source energy, and my True Self, I feel a sense of security that cannot be extinguished by any kind of loss. It is sturdy, stable, and durable. Feeling anchored to self and the forces for good who want to help me is where the prospect of change becomes less intimidating. I am safe to faithfully persevere, knowing the way through something is to go *through* it as many times as I have to until I reach the other side. That motivational energy was present the entire trip, and I found the courage to merge with it.

Now I needed to learn how to live it.

At last, I made the decision to deal with unexpressed grief going back as far as I could recall, witnessing with startling clarity the unconscious thought pattern of generational dysfunction that ran my life. Suffering from pain and pushing it down into the hole that grew bigger with each unhealed traumatic loss, I began to grieve it all: the death of my grandparents, my mother's breast cancer diagnosis, the pain of my parents' unstable marriage, the infidelity, their divorce, losing a touch more of my self-respect with each drunken demoralization of my body. I grieved the devastation of our hometown after Hurricane Sandy, my boyfriend Mike's death, the loss of identity that presented after moving to Colorado, the five family members who died within three years of our move, and my sexual trauma.

Rumi, the thirteenth-century Persian poet and Sufi mystic, stated: "Yesterday I was clever, so I wanted to change the world. Today I am wise, so I am changing myself." That's exactly what I did, and I achieved it by healing my grief, then healing my marriage. But first, I had to face and accept a few hard truths.

The experience in Seattle exposed, in a most brutal and crushing way, that I wasn't allowing myself to love Jim wholeheartedly and with abandon. I loved him but didn't know how to be in love with him, how to meet him in love. I was afraid of it. Truth be told, the feeling of security that comes from being united with another human was never there to be crushed in the first place. The insecure state of our marriage didn't pop up standing in a crowd at a rock concert. It had been the case all along, but I could not see it. If I wanted to move forward with healing my marriage, I had to understand I subconsciously picked up on traits in Jim that kept me in a constant state of emotional abandonment. I had to accept I set this ball in motion.

Early in our relationship, Jim feared vulnerability like I did. This meant he wouldn't force me into the uncomfortable space I wanted to avoid. I was safe in my armor because emotional intimacy wasn't offered. This dynamic worked for me until it didn't. I don't know exactly when it changed, but I needed and wanted emotional intimacy, yet I could not receive it from Jim. When he attempted to enter this sacred space with me after Jeremy died by sitting beside me as I cried, reaching out to embrace me and asking to talk, I was checked out. I physically moved away from him when he sat down on the bed next to me. I had made the decision years before I couldn't get what I needed from him, so I could not accept his offer now. It felt wrong.

My brother's death confirmed my personal narrative, The Great Myth: everyone will leave me or hurt me. The world and the people in it cannot be trusted, and pain is around the corner waiting to devour me, so I must protect myself at all costs. My life experiences compounded The Great Myth, and Jeremy's death made it true. I was never going to suffer another agonizing loss like that, becoming debilitated where all I could do for months was lie in bed, take a bath, go to my recovery groups, and cry. I was not going to love so deeply and be pained so badly that I could not take care of my children and myself. Our survival had been threatened, and I would never risk that again. Nope, not ever. So, I hardened my heart and rambled forward, unknowingly destroying everything around me including my relationship with Jim.

Time and lots of digging, sifting, more digging, and more sifting exposed the truth about my marriage. I manifested The Great

Myth by unconsciously making a choice to protect myself. I had no idea my mind was conspiring for self-preservation. Ironically, that self-preservation did not self-preserve at all; it did the exact opposite. It protected my heart by ravaging my soul.

I shut out my husband emotionally and spiritually against my soul's desire for connection and began grieving our marriage. I couldn't bear the thought of more loss should Jim die before me.

I wanted to get the mourning over with while I was already in it.

It's true nothing of value comes easy. They say the hardest part of anything is to begin, and that's also true. Before we could begin to heal, Jim and I had to become aware of the tricks our minds were playing on us. Calling forth the courage to admit the truth about who we were and the families we descended from, we got honest with ourselves and each other about our individual failings and our pain. Then we got honest about why we chose one another.

Sitting in Tracy's office, eyes brimming with tears, we began to see how sick we both were when we met and how neither of us knew it. To be fair to Jim, I was at the top of my game right after celebrating my first year in recovery. It's called newcomer fire, and I had it. My grasp and implementation of the twelve steps were admirable, and I was helping a lot of women get sober. My husband saw my flair and was attracted to my commitment to recovery. What he didn't see was I was grieving Mike ... hard. Mike died five months before my first date with Jim. (Jeremy died five months before the attraction in Seattle. Do I see a pattern?) Grief-stricken, lost, and insecure, I was a mess but presented otherwise. I appeared like I had my life together, like I was thriving, when really I was a damsel in distress seeking a savior to lift me out of despair. Jim was seeking a damsel to save.

With Tracy's help, we unpacked our limiting belief systems about life and love and saw we had been casting doubt and fear at one another, the result of living with the pain of unresolved issues. She showed us how we sporadically addressed these issues but stuffed them back into boxes when it got too heavy, packing them away to sort through at a later date. When that later date arrived, we would look again, briefly, before packing them away once more. It was a continual cycle of satisfaction and despair. We had to come clean about the merry-go-round we were on and that we thought was normal, telling ourselves and each other this is how marriage is.

Finally, we became willing to unpack all the boxes until they were empty. Literally. Tracy drew boxes on a piece of paper and we labeled them: intimacy (mental, emotional, spiritual, and physical), grief, trauma, money, trust, connection, children, extended family, career, and more. She helped us explore the boxes honestly and vulnerably.

We talked about The Great Myth and learned how my limiting belief system about marriage recreated the cold distance of my parents' relationship. My resentment of Jim's illnesses and his character flaws (or survival traits) faded upon admitting I projected my generational dysfunction onto him and our family. Expecting the same experience I had as a child, I unconsciously reconstructed a similar environment: a home of anxiety and perfectionism. Jim's trauma and his need for a controlled environment aided me well in this. We were both unaware he suffered from PTSD until well into our marriage, yet the characteristics of his illness were attractive to me because it allowed me to live in anxiety (both my own and his), then use perfectionism to make it go away. The sick behavior of creating a problem to solve or enhancing a tense situation created by Jim so I could fix it was my vehicle to gain self-worth. I fixed the problem and made the anxiety go away; therefore, I was good. Jim saw how his beliefs played out negatively in our marriage too.

Once aware of our behavior, we became willing to meet each other's needs and to change ourselves by fixing character flaws that kept us endlessly yearning for satisfaction, both as a couple and personally. That's the beauty of Imago Therapy: changing the parts of myself responsible for Jim's unmet needs is the process that filled the void in my "lost self." Take emotional intimacy, for example: as I learn to become emotionally intimate with Jim, I heal the place in me that fears intimacy. Now let's look at perfectionism: My unrealistic expectations set the bar unattainably high for Jim, demanding him to constantly produce and produce well. Healing this flaw by maintaining realistic expectations for myself removes the pressure placed on him, reduces stress in our relationship, and helps me go easy on myself.

Both my fear of emotional intimacy and the need to be perfect stem from my umbrella issue: feelings of inadequacy. Healing feelings of inadequacy by validating my self-worth creates an emotionally secure attachment to my being, naturally resulting in a closer, fulfilling marriage in which I am safe to love.

After doing the work on ourselves to become emotionally secure, Jim and I gifted each other pure love. No longer living in painful yet familiar feelings of abandonment that create separation, we meet in the sacred space of unity. We do not act to complete the other anymore. Rather, we engage in mutual caring made possible by caring for ourselves. Instead of two empty people trying to meet each other's needs and having nothing to give, we meet our own needs and this self-sufficiency organically leads to healthy interdependence. There is not one caregiver and care-receiver; we are both caregivers and care-receivers. I meet my own needs and Jim's needs. He meets his own and mine.

Now when I hear the garage door open signaling Jim is home, I feel excited. We turn up the tunes and the dancing continues as we welcome him into the fold, on the good days. On the challenging days, I remember we are human and will always have work to do to stay emotionally secure and spiritually fit.

If you are unhappy in your marriage and have a desire to dig deeper, go to marriage counseling, read the Imago book, and use the accompanying Imago workbook before you make a major decision. The gamut of marital issues runs deep, and this process may not save your marriage, but it's worth the effort if you walk away confidently knowing you turned over every stone. It's also smart to engage in this work before you get married.

If it doesn't work out, you still grew closer to your True Being, closer to whole. You took a step toward trusting yourself and being all in.

14

BREAKING
THE CURSE

My experience in Seattle was never about another person, nor was it about Jim. It was about me and my soul lesson, a spiritual awakening. My spirit gang presented an opportunity to look at why I never felt settled in my skin, and to do so by breaking the curse.

The leader of the pack, Jeremy, showed up through a kindred spirit. (After all, he said he wouldn't miss Pearl Jam playing in his backyard!) Highly attuned to the soulful energy of the crowd and grieving intensely, I felt him through another. Desperate to hold on to Jeremy's energy, colliding with my unhappy marriage, I attached myself to this intimate emotional and spiritual connection. Letting go of this energy brought forth the part of my soul that needed healing and encouraged me to address the source of my pain—all my pain.

Week after week after week, I poured my heart out to Tracy. She knew exactly what to say, exactly when it needed to be said. She challenged me to get real about The Great Myth, and to go deep to understand how it played out in past romantic relationships.

Suffering from emotional abandonment and fearing loss, I unconsciously hurt others to push them away, especially after I found out about Dad's affair with our "aunt." I broke a lot of hearts that summer, committing acts similar to those of my dad. Cheating on a boyfriend with one of my best friend's ex-boyfriends, I lost two relationships in one fell swoop (and a waitressing job because I was too hungover to work the next day).

Relationships were not frivolous to me; they were sacred. But I did whatever I needed to do to feel wanted and sought that feeling whenever and wherever I could. My fear of abandonment was stronger than my ability to be faithful.

Breaking down the false narrative I had told myself for thirty-eight years, I understood how and why I acted the way I did with friends and family members: Why I wanted the invitation to the party I didn't want to go to. Why I entered conversations expecting to be hurt. Why I chose a set of three girlfriends to pal around with, so I could feel left out. I wanted to be wanted but I could not accept the feeling when offered, so I sabotaged it. I ruined relationships before they ruined me. My low self-worth told me I deserved to be abandoned, so I unconsciously created rejection even though I was petrified of it. Loss is often unpredictable, so I kept myself in a habitual state of abandonment in an attempt to control it. If I was going to be abandoned, I was going to be the one doing the abandoning! It seemed less painful to live this way.

By admitting I carry this pain, looking at where it stems from, and doing the work to heal, I break the family curse of generational dysfunction. I'm not a bad person, and neither is my father or the other family members who fell prey to the lie. I was a sick person, suffering from The Great Myth. The difference between me and those who came before me in my family is the generation I was born into. It's about timing and a shift in mindset. I benefit from the evolution of consciousness taking place now that helps me understand the problem and gives me permission to heal.

After this initial healing, I was able to tackle my sexual trauma.

Four years into the most recent round of therapy, I began EFT (Emotional Freedom Technique) tapping to heal the inner wounds that desecrated my young soul. In this treatment, Tracy leads me through a series of taps and phrases to describe the negative, neutral, and positive perspectives of these traumas. I do not minimize my experiences. I make peace with the memories.

Tapping on meridian points, I move energy (or chi, as it's called in Eastern medicine), signaling the brain to calm down. As the energy moves and my brain begins to de-stress, I reframe what happened. A series of eye movements, breathing, and humming solidifies this new thinking.

Experiencing a physiological change, I no longer retreat into myself when I recall traumatic memories or when I think about intimacy with Jim, physically and emotionally. I've stopped pulling away ever so slightly when he hugs me. I now lean in when approached and even initiate physical connection. Feeling safe and comfortable, intimacy is no longer a chore to be endured. Emotionally, I feel less anxious sharing my innermost thoughts with Jim and look forward to our nightly conversations after the kids go to bed. Our relationship is more stimulating on every level.

This work was not comfortable, but it worked and continues to work when we make the effort. Our connection is stable underneath the mess that occasionally appears. When it does, we use the tools we have been taught to tackle the mess before it turns into a disaster. And when disaster strikes, we pull out the big guns and really get to it. Whether that means confiding in closed-mouthed, trusted friends to seek guidance, learning a new therapeutic technique, or taking space to sort out our feelings, we do it. Pride and anger may stall us for more time than is advisable, but we eventually access the help we need, individually and together. We are both blessed with a willingness to listen to the inner urge and to follow the compulsion toward progressing in a better direction.

One example is the time we took our annual summer vacation to Long Beach in July 2021. Leery of Jim returning to the hot spot of his trauma, where his PTSD fuse is lit, I originally planned the trip for just me and my daughters. We had decided family trips to New York are not good for Jim's mental health or for our relationship. After three days of arguing and of him assuring me EMDR changed him, I acquiesced.

The beginning of the week was as smooth as the sea breeze coming through the window of the hotel we stayed in on the boardwalk, the site of our wedding reception. To our delight, the EMDR worked. On the fourth day, a vehicle speeding toward a stop sign on the corner of the street we were crossing sparked a reaction in Jim, causing a huge scene. Given our young daughters were privy to another outburst that put them in a dangerous situation, I was furious and in great despair. Ready to end our marriage, I called a friend and she talked me out of it. After a full afternoon of smoke streaming from my ears, I calmed down.

Having knowledge about Jim's condition and compassion for the uncontrollable emotions and actions that accompany post-traumatic stress, I decided I wasn't ready to give up on us. After a painstaking conversation imploring him to seek further treatment, he agreed. A few months later he began Rapid Resolution Therapy (RRT), a hypnotherapy that uses symbols, metaphors, and visuals to reprocess traumatic memories lodged in the limbic system. This type of reprocessing works to rewire neural pathways and synapses in the brain, which in turn regulate the nervous system. Three sessions of hypnotherapy brought more healing than years of talk therapy and a year of EMDR, although the dramatic change may have been heightened because he underwent those therapies first. Meditation, an important and effective tool in our recovery program, also aided in how much success Jim had with RRT. He was primed for the multilevel healing that took place.

I also stepped up my game when it became obvious I need something more to enhance my wellness. Unwilling to continue living with an above average level of anxiety, I too engaged in RRT in late 2022. Life still hits, but my anxiety has been greatly diminished in light of my problems and a stabilizing calm has taken its place. In addition, I seek help in the mood-supplement section of the health food store. I've finally admitted I have a chemical imbalance.

A natural serotonin boost gives me what I need to function as a person with a normal serotonin level. It doesn't give me more than I need; it provides me with the amount necessary to supplement my deficiency.

We keep going back to the wellspring of health because our family and our lives depend on it. As recovered alcoholics, where pain holds the power to kill, we cannot afford to sit in resentment for too long. As parents, we cannot afford to stay downhearted because our unhappiness bleeds out to the children. As a couple, we choose not to stay discontented because we deserve comfort and love.

We deserve to break the curse.

15

A MISSION TO UNDERSTAND

Self-centered fear is the number one ego-driven determinant of misunderstanding and resentment. This wildly popular trademark of fear, and the subsequent emotional selfishness it commands, erodes relationships with more intensity than a vicious tornado ripping through the Great Plains.

Our egos (you know—the ones out in the parking lot doing push-ups) are snuggled up next to self-centered fear doing partner relays. There is no surprise the two are closely linked, for one inflames the other. Once we feel the tiniest trace of fear, our egos promptly shift into overdrive in a desperate attempt to feel safe. Defenses are raised, often creating emotionally charged situations that lead to resentment.

Let's look at the driver who cuts you off. The fear of an accident precipitates the ego response: hands in the air, shouting expletives, and maybe even flipping the bird if you're feeling extra feisty. But when we cut people off, 99 percent of the time absentmindedly, we expect them to understand and forgive us. We all make mistakes. So why do we have such a hard time responding in kind?

The double standard of expecting people to forgive us for a slight but throwing daggers when they slight us is not conducive to trustworthy connection. We have to make a decision whether we're going to universally forgive human errors or if we expect people to let us off the hook without returning the nicety. Think about your current beliefs and relationships. Do you expect to be loved, understood, and forgiven under all conditions but your love, understanding, and forgiveness is conditional, especially when you don't agree with what is said or done?

Jesus's lesson from Luke 6:31, "Do to others as you would have them do to you" exemplifies this concept. This sensible idea has been sorely neglected through the centuries. Have we ever practiced this beautiful sentiment of mutual respect on a mass scale or is it just a trite phrase we teach to first graders? Is this lack of reciprocation responsible for most resentment?

If we do not practice unconditional love and understanding, self-centered fear (ego) takes the podium as victor with a gold medal around its perfidious neck. At that point, hope for trust and connection is decimated and we remain bitter and isolated. Relationships, and civilization at large, surely will not budge in the right direction.

Deep-rooted, familial resentment is the most damaging resentment. Far-reaching and growing stronger over time, it can keep us in a chronic state of disconnection from the masses. We may take resentment toward parents, siblings, or children and adapt it as a worldview, creating distrust in daily situations and other relationships.

If I leave my house smoldering over a troubling conversation with a family member, firm in resentment (most likely dating back decades) and in righteousness, do you think I'm going to have pleasant interactions with the people I meet along my way? Probably not. I'm more likely to project my exasperation onto the innocent humans encountered while traveling my route. They will seem oppositional because I am feeling oppositional. I let one conversation ruin both my morning and the mornings of members of my community. Returning home, I am more upset than I was before I left my house.

Resentment is powerful. Generating a spiral of negativity, destructive energy released into the universe echoes in the ethers, intensifies, then reverberates as more destructive energy.

Why do we hold such grudges? We do it to protect ourselves from the pain of being wrong, to strengthen the ego. We create stories partly based in truth, but exaggerated, and we use the fantastical stories as a tool to massage our egos. It feels good to be right—so good. But after a few days, pride turns to anger and we are left feeling unseen and unheard. We feel this way because we cannot see or hear the one we are holding a grudge against and we lack trust they will see or hear us.

One can rightly assume this lack of understanding and distrust further widens the wedge; divisiveness closes our hearts and minds. Stretching our emotional distance, irrational assumptions run riot and resentment grows. At best, we agree to disagree, to maintain whatever amount of respect we have left for each other. We decide this is the mature thing to do, while resentment lies dormant under the pretense and the division grows wider. The mature thing to do is to listen and seek to understand, to see and hear one another as fellow sufferers of the human experience. Ideally, we end the conversation feeling respect for our differences, trust intact.

I have tried approaching stressful conversations with the mission to understand, admittedly not often enough, and the times I did, the interaction went well, or at least better than when entering it resentfully. I've also entered hard conversations with a positive intention and didn't like what I heard. I listened anyway, bit my tongue at moments, and by the end of the conversation something changed and I left feeling better. Carole, the great sage she is, tells me to write KMS on my palm when entering these difficult conversations. It stands for "keep mouth shut." Surprisingly, it works. When my mouth is shut, I can listen. Listening leads to understanding and understanding leads to trust.

Understanding does not mean agreeing. It means you are willing to learn how capable someone is of showing love. Be willing to broaden your perspective, your idea of what their love looks like. Strive to understand the capacity in which they can emit love. It may be in ways you think you cannot receive, but that doesn't mean it isn't there. Some people show love through gifts, others through acts of service or compliments. If you are willing to get creative, you will start to notice it and over time you will begin to absorb it.

Our main mission during our current incarnation is to defy resentment as often as possible and to love ourselves and others (sometimes from afar) no matter how offended we are. It is imperative we forbid dark energy to divide us. You do not have to give your lower nature airtime (unless you are consciously doing shadow work). Do not join it when it arrives out of the blue, either direct from you or from others you meet along your journey.

Beat the resentment back by sending it healing heart energy.

The opposite of emotional selfishness is emotional selflessness. St. Francis of Assisi is known for one of the most timeless and humble prayers for learning to live with emotional selflessness. Offering highly effectual guidelines, this prayer keeps the ego in check when our emotions want to get the best of us.

The prayer hangs on my dining room wall in a black eighteen-by-twenty-four-inch frame. Strategically hung, it attracts my glances frequently while I'm standing in front of my bottomless coffee pot. It's on a small card tucked into the side of my china cabinet, and it's in the meditation cave. It's printed on one of my bookmarks. I can't say enough about it. It goes like this:

> Lord, make me an instrument of your peace.
> Where there is hatred, let me sow love;
> where there is injury, pardon;
> where there is doubt, faith;
> where there is despair, hope;
> where there is darkness, light;
> where there is sadness, joy.

O Divine Master,
grant that I may not so much seek
to be consoled, as to console;
to be understood, as to understand;
to be loved, as to love.
For it is in giving that we receive;
it is in pardoning that we are pardoned;
and it is in dying that we are born to eternal life.
Amen.

Attributed to Catholicism, this prayer goes way beyond the church doors. Emotional struggle within our hearts and when dealing with other humans breaks the barriers of any religious institution. I wouldn't call it a Catholic prayer—it's a human prayer. If you aren't down with formal prayer, try looking at it as a set of directions.

In the first part, St. Francis gives us specific words to focus on while attempting to shift from ego to love, from self to spirit, from emotional selfishness to selflessness. When hatred crops up, we try to feel love; when doubt creeps in, we look for faith; when in despair, we search for hope. The second part is remarkably useful for entering tough interactions, for seeking to understand the behaviors and actions of the most troublesome folks. When I am trying to understand instead of trying to be understood, the focus is not on my emotional needs. It's on how I can best serve others, the key to emotional selflessness.

This prayer saved my relationship with my mother after I moved to Colorado. She was devastated when we broke the news we were moving. Inviting her to come with us, I tried to convince her it was a good thing. Whenever I did, she moved slightly further away from me emotionally, as she was preparing herself for major loss—she knew she would never move to Colorado. Plus, she was incredibly hurt by our decision. I was taking her daughter and grandbabies away. Now both of her children and three grandchildren would live across the country. The more distant she got, the more I pushed. My guilt was eating at me: if I could get her to move with us, I wouldn't be a lousy daughter for leaving. Trying to change how she felt to assuage my guilt only induced guilty feelings for her. She wondered where her maternal instincts were, why she didn't want to follow us out west. She felt alone and abandoned and could not understand why she wasn't enough for us to stay in New York. She was. It was just time to leave.

Consumed with self-centered fear that I ruined our relationship, I could not see how much pain I caused by moving far away. My focus was on how she did not support our move and how she hurt me, yet I judged myself harshly for leaving. It was a catch-22, and my words and actions reflected this confusion and hurt.

Judging myself, I judged her for lack of support. Feeling judged, she pulled away. When the pain became great enough, I made a decision I would see things from her perspective. I would stop trying to convince her how wonderful our move was. Instead, I would meet her in her pain. I begged my Higher Power to relieve me of self-judgment and to help me see that her reaction was not about me. I was not a lousy daughter for moving; she was hurt because she felt abandoned and it was not my responsibility to heal that. This perspective was hard to move from my head to my heart, and I needed help from a source much bigger than me.

Focusing intently on each line of the St. Francis prayer, I considered how to become a person who truly embodied the message. I felt the pain: mine and hers. Then I imagined the healing that might occur if I put this prayer into action, if I tried to understand how she felt, and only how she felt. Instead of seeking to be understood, I sought to understand by putting myself in her shoes, with patience and compassion. It took years, but I started acting with patience and compassion when around her. The lack of pressure to change resulted in her not feeling judged. She felt seen, heard, and loved unconditionally. Feeling this way, she was able to give me the love and support I needed. I could have reduced years of pain for both of us if I was able to do this from the start. But hey, it takes what it takes.

Emotional selflessness is evident when other people's actions do not hit on a personal level. "Where there is injury, pardon" sums up this emotionally mature idea. Quick to overlook a harm, you do not take offense. You are free to pardon another's behavior because that person's actions do not affect you—neither the oversight nor the intentional infraction. Consider the example of the car cutting you off for no good reason. The driver cut you off because he felt like cutting you off. There was no reasonable explanation, yet you do not become disturbed. You are not injured. You're okay, knowing the driver was not thinking about you, only himself. You do not feel slighted because you know it's not about you. Emotionally mature, you don't take it personally.

Ridding yourself of emotional selfishness is easy to do when you realize everything is not all about you, all the time.

In fact, nothing is.

Six months into my COVID-19 hiatus, a Zoom coffee date with a good friend found me releasing my angst about the state of the world. (Angst is not reserved only for teenagers.) I was full of frustration and seeking solace, and my sentient friend offered me a mantra to repeat. Finally, I was able to put a name to the spiritual endowment of good vibes I had been offering humanity all those years. She told me it is called Metta meditation, an established Buddhist meditation. This is what Colleen suggested when she told me to visualize the people of the world circled up, holding hands, and sharing love. (I've since added animals to our circle!)

These are the exact words my friend gave me. The wording is optional, but the sincerity is not:

May I be happy.
May I be healthy.
May I know freedom.
May I walk the world with ease.

This meditation is commonly practiced by sending the healing message to yourself first, then to those you love, then to acquaintances: the mom you see every day at school pickup, the bagger at the grocery store, the doorman at your office building. Then, send this message to perfect strangers. And then, importantly, send it to those who disturb you or are your perceived adversaries.

Some people start with the most burdensome people and work their way back to themselves. I find it effective to start with me. I must practice self-love by giving myself good wishes before I can genuinely give love and good wishes to others.

When sending this healing energy to other people, change the "I" to "they"

May they be happy.
May they be healthy.
May they know freedom.
May they walk the world with ease.

Metta meditation teaches us how to open the disenchanted, rusty gates of our hearts, how to break the chains that keep us penned in the jail of distrust and separation. We let light in and give it out. We feel it return to our heart centers, then send it out again, creating then reinforcing a Ring of Love. Whereas my heart and your heart were isolated in separate spaces of fear and judgment, the circle of light closes, merging its dismembered pieces. We become one in common suffering, common love, and common healing. We trust in our oneness, our thoughts and actions connected in goodwill, and this sense of security allows us to feel safe to be all in with our entire human family.

Metta meditation is a wheel of high-frequency, powerful healing energy, a path to freedom that may feel curious at the start but works.

Give it a go. It just may free your soul.

16

THE HOLY GRAIL

I forgive Jeremy for not treating his addiction, for putting our family through pain, and for leaving his daughter to navigate the world fatherless. I forgive my dad for breaking our family apart, for not knowing how to do better. I forgive my "aunt" for pushing my mother into all-consuming grief so incapacitating that she was unable to help Jeremy and me in the way we needed to be helped. I forgive that woman because she must have been suffering a great deal to harm her best friend—like I was the times I cheated on my boyfriends or when I found myself at a rock concert seeking a connection with someone I thought could relieve me of my pain. I forgive those who sexually traumatized me. Most likely it happened to them in some capacity.

I reached this state by practicing Compassion Forgiveness.

Compassion Forgiveness involves releasing the other person from blame by sincerely believing they did the best they could, based on their mental, emotional, and spiritual capacity as a result of learned experience. This is the gist of Luke 23:34, "Father, forgive them, for they know not what they do." The state of Metta meditation is an excellent time to practice Compassion Forgiveness. As I send love to others, I discern whether I can hold people responsible for actions that hurt me if they are suffering the pangs of their own painful experiences.

Can I be upset with somebody for trauma that was inflicted upon them and for their unskilled reaction? Can I justify a resentment if they've been so hurt that they are programmed to be who they are and cannot change, if they've never been taught how to change or simply do not see the need for change? Does someone require forgiveness if they are constitutionally unable to do better?

Those who continue to hurt others are suffering. All people have love and light in their hearts. All humans are born with it. Have you ever held a baby and thought, "This baby is evil?" I hope not. Love and light get buried under piles of difficulty and trauma. Taking this view means we no longer blame said person. We place blame on a force stronger than people's ability to alter their perspective and choose a better way due to faulty thinking patterns passed down through generations and cemented in childhood. We understand they are suffering, like us.

Does the typical idea of forgiveness become irrelevant when we look at it this way? Forgiveness may be irrelevant as it relates to releasing others (lack of resentment means there is nothing to forgive) but it surely matters when it comes to our personal emotional freedom. We still need to do our inner work to heal.

Compassion Forgiveness may seem like capitulation—giving in to bad behavior or accepting poor treatment from another. That is not so. The person is not exonerated. We aren't accepting bad behavior or turning the other cheek. We are trying to understand someone's actions by believing those actions were most likely beyond that person's control.

This way of thinking is for us, not the other person. Holding onto resentment gives the perceived assailant power over us. Open hearts may close, and the pain of a closed heart can force behavior we aren't proud of. If we then create pain for others, the cycle continues. When we practice Compassion Forgiveness, we choose limitless love. We break the chains of dysfunction and set ourselves free.

Compassion Forgiveness is a tricky position to take in the parent-child relationship. Children (including some adult children) expect parents to act with pure selflessness one hundred percent of the time. This is unrealistic, yet the natural dynamic exists. Parents, being human, have limitations due to their personal natures and social environments, past and present. At some point, they fall from the pedestal of perfection like a star resting precariously atop a Christmas tree touched ever so slightly. Unable to reconcile a parent's action, the child is left disillusioned and hurt. The pain is almost impossible to reckon with as a child, so many carry it into adulthood.

Roles do not matter in our ability to love another. We returned to this delicate, yet stable, sphere as spiritual beings choosing different roles to play throughout our lives, but those roles do not define how humble, far, or wide our love can grow.

Can you move past humanly constructed roles and how we are supposed to play them? Will you look upon everyone—parents, grandparents, siblings, teachers—as tender souls here to learn and grow from each other regardless of age, status, or life experience? Have you considered maybe the adult child is here to love the parent like the parent needs to be loved? Parents, have you considered your children may teach you more than you will teach them? The hierarchy of roles and the associated assumptions, as well as the restrictions of those roles, are equalized when you think about it this way. This attitude is the main ingredient in Compassion Forgiveness.

We are called to be changemakers, and it begins by understanding that much dysfunction we see today is perpetuated unconsciously and passed down through generations. This does not give anyone a pass—accountability is necessary to curb the dysfunction—but we can choose to look upon those who hurt others with understanding and compassion.

It's time to put an end to the painful narrative of our lives, to stop the blame game and focus on how we can change ourselves by shifting our perspectives. When the old stories are revised, new messages hold the power to heal deep wounds.

Let nothing stop you from this grave undertaking you are called to do. Be a warrior of healing for yourself, your family, and the world.

The term "toxic," when used to describe people, doesn't sit well with me. Formaldehyde is toxic; anthrax is toxic; people are not toxic. A person who treats another poorly is suffering from an emotional maladjustment, not toxicity.

Calling someone toxic is an unwise ego-feed. If I decide someone is toxic instead of suffering, I not only place myself above that person but I shy away, impairing my ability to grow through our interaction, however extensive or limited that may be.

I used to think kindness toward somebody who was unkind to me was inauthentic, that remaining in that person's presence demonstrated a lack of self-respect and I was not honoring my boundaries. Naturally, I avoided people who were unkind to me. Mistaken in my handling of a troubled soul, I now know remaining in proximity to a challenging person is not inauthentic. Avoidance is more self-protection and self-abandonment, a dishonoring of my soul's mission to be love. The most authentic thing I can do is show up in my heart space, as myself, regardless of what people are doing around me. (Again, I am speaking of difficult relationships, not abuse.) I do not have to reduce myself to act in a way I am uncomfortable with to meet people on their level. Neither do you. We can stand strong in love, with strong boundaries.

Like loss and hardship, adversaries are often our greatest teachers if we look for the opportunities. They give us the chance to evolve emotionally and spiritually. We do not have to subject ourselves to their presence often or ever. Some people are energy suckers and leave us feeling worn out. We get to choose if we want to engage with them. We also get to choose if we want to put forth the effort required to change for the sake of the relationship, to give love when it's hard. We can feel the difference between jumping ship because we are unwilling to change our behavior versus fleeing because it's destructive to our well-being. Trust that feeling.

Boundary-setting is an alternative to complete disengagement. If this is the path we choose, we can orchestrate communication that supports our pursuit of spiritual growth. We can make use of our pain.

Difficult relationships can feel like riding a hamster wheel, an exhausting cycle that goes nowhere. We often think we have to ride the wheel or vacate the cage. We don't have to do either. If we choose to stay, we can recreate boundaries true to our values while others are true to theirs, somewhere in the middle. This is a space of compromise that works for us. It's the space of Esteemable Boundaries. Extending patience, compassion, and understanding despite the unsavory behavior exhibited by others grows our self-esteem and strengthens our commitment to be love. It's far from easy, but this is where our power lies if we choose to stay in the relationship (or do not have the option to leave, such as with a coworker).

Others may respect our boundaries and remain in the cage with us. They may not. If they do not, and we inquire but they are unwilling to hash it out, we can let it be. Closure is not a requirement for letting go. Buttoning up is not necessary or even desired, for letting the frayed edges hang out enhances endurance for living with uncertainty. And as we've learned, living with uncertainty is a useful skill for building trust in ourselves, especially when the threat of loss is present.

If a person is willing to remain in the cage with us, great. The following path to Esteemable Boundaries helps us redefine our perspective of that person and the relationship: We can think of the person as a child, in his or her actual childhood. We can imagine the child's pain. If we are privy to the person's history, all the better. Now we can wrap our arms around this hurting child who needs love. We can give this person what he or she longs for, energetically.

I did this with my mom while trying to heal our fractured relationship after the move. I imagined her as a young girl and tried to feel what life was like for her growing up in the 1960s—a ten-year-old at home with her parents, both sisters living on their own. I pictured Grandma Tessie mopping the floors, hanging laundry on the line, or cooking ziti as mom played jacks alone, as she often found herself. Putting my arms around her, I told her she isn't alone and she is worth my time and attention. She smiled wide at me. I picked up the small rubber ball and we began playing, laughing, and enjoying each other's company.

Practice this for a while, and you will find compassion for what drives another's hurtful behavior. The shackles of your mind break, and the portal of your heart opens as you choose to maintain and boost allegiance to your light, to *the* light. You become free to show up in love (and to retreat when necessary), on your terms. Esteemable Boundaries built from self-respect and compassion are easy to set.

Trusting yourself to be all in, not with the other person but with your commitment to compassion, you are safe to love and let go. This way of life is high up on the ladder of emotional evolution and spiritual ascension.

It's the holy grail.

17

SELF-COMPASSION

It's a spiritual axiom that we cannot forgive others until we forgive ourselves. I can try to forgive you, but my pain will interfere. My experiences are colored by my perception, and my perception is created by how I feel about myself. If my heart is closed off to me, I cannot open it to you.

So give yourself a nice, big hug. Right now. Put the book down. Wrap your arms around yourself and say, *I love you. I forgive you.* Please don't wait as long as I did to forgive yourself for your mistakes. It was a long road of learning how to love myself, and I arrived by practicing self-compassion.

The concept of sin has provoked me since I sat in the pew at my Roman Catholic Church, preparing to take my first Holy Communion in second grade. How could I be a sinner without committing a sinful act? Didn't I have to do something wrong to be a sinner? It didn't make sense, and I didn't like the idea one bit.

Then it came to me. The priest was right. I was a sinner.

My communion happened shortly after my second sexually traumatic event. The feeling that I was bad, dirty, and shameful allowed the priest's words to play nicely into The Great Myth taking shape at this time of my life. Not only did his words coincide with my thought process but they reinforced it. I *deserved* for people to hurt me because I was bad, dirty, and shameful. I *deserved* to be hurt because I was a sinner.

Years later, I questioned the concept of sin again.

The day after I returned home from Seattle, we attended church as a family. I was a mess but went because I was scheduled to run the sound board. Showing up for my commitment in a haze, I pushed microphone switches, praying muscle memory would pull me through. Intermittently, I stared at the back of Jim's head and watched my daughters fidget in their seats. I wondered if I would burst into flames right there in the sanctuary, not because I felt guilty, but because I didn't feel guilty. My sinful thoughts confirmed my guilt, but I could not bring myself to feel bad about having those thoughts. They felt natural, real, and human.

I came home from the concert with emotions I was powerless to change. Sensing this was part of a bigger plan, like these feelings arose to serve a great purpose, I wondered how they could be sinful. A church friend helped me sort it out. She explained the word "sin" in Greek means mistake. That's all—a mistake. Not a scarlet letter, not a damnation to hell—a mistake. And how do mistakes help us? They help us learn and grow.

As an active alcoholic, I made more mistakes than I can recall due to numerous blackouts. But without the mistakes that caused me and others immense pain, I would not have sought a spiritual way of life in recovery, one that compels me to heal. If I didn't make a mistake by nurturing what I felt in Seattle, I wouldn't have done the work to become the woman of self-worth, self-love, and self-compassion I am today. Jim and I most likely could have birthed a new relationship without the pain, but I'm not sure either of us would have done so with as much grit if divorce was not in our headlights.

I am not condoning hurting others. I do condone forgiving yourself for thoughts and feelings you are powerless to control. Give yourself grace to investigate what's underneath the thoughts and feelings, then ask your Higher Power for courage to look in the mirror, seek the truth, and heal.

Turns out sinning has been my greatest teacher.

While I was in the depths of despair after the concert, my oldest brother Jason told me about a Hawaiian mantra used to forgive ourselves and others by clearing current and ancestral baggage we carry. A meditation practice of reconciliation with self, those who are alive, and those who've passed, Ho'oponopono, which translates to "to make right," opens the gates of self-compassion. This mantra breaks the chains keeping us tied to pain. Here it is:

I am sorry.
Please forgive me.
Thank you.
I love you.[4]

In the book *Zero Limits* by Joe Vitale, the author describes a "cleaning" method learned from his spiritual teacher, Ihaleakala Hew Len, PhD. Dr. Hew Len tells the story of how he healed patients in a locked ward for the criminally insane by healing his own energy through a process called "Self I-dentity." Sending himself love and forgiveness, as expressed in this mantra, he took 100 percent responsibility for "cleaning" the energy within himself. (Turns out I was onto something with my incessant cleaning. I was just cleaning the wrong things.) He then showered the inmates with the same energy from afar. The healing took place despite the doctor's lack of proximity to the inmates.

That's all he did. He did not perform therapy. He did not sit in on groups or staff meetings. He took responsibility for healing his own energy, then he sent that good energy to the inmates, and it worked.

Hermes Trismegistus, known as the Greek god of interpretive communication (a combination of the Greek god, Hermes, and Thoth, the Egyptian god of wisdom) is known to have said, "As above, so below, as within, so without, as the universe, so the soul ..." This is the same idea demonstrated by Dr. Hew Len: healing myself heals you. We do this by cleansing past memories that shape our thought patterns today. As with grief and emotional abandonment, it doesn't matter if your feelings and perceptions of past events are accurate because it's true for you and affects your actions now.

The first phrase in the Ho'oponopono mantra is, "I am sorry." We are taking responsibility for the events that happened in our life because of negative perceptions or conditioned responses. We are not apologizing to another person; we are compassionately apologizing to our Higher Self and to the universe for not knowing any better and, therefore, being unable to do better. We are also apologizing for knowing the correct path and choosing the low road anyway.

The next part is, "Please forgive me." As we ask for forgiveness from the universe for both conscious and unconscious behavior, we are careful not to demonize ourselves, as that would lower our vibration and make this work harder to achieve—or worse, make it null. We simply recognize our own mistakes and the mistakes of our ancestors (whether we know about them or not) and earnestly seek forgiveness for all.

By saying "thank you," we express gratitude to the universe for the loving-kindness it consistently grants us and for cleansing our negative energy. We also thank the universe for allowing our current incarnation on Earth, for our physical vessels given to us as mechanisms for healing.

The last phrase is, "I love you." Feeling deeply what it means to be love, we let it warm us to our core. As we become pure love, we open our hearts and send genuine adoration to our Higher Self and to creation.

The more heartfelt you speak the Ho'oponopono mantra, the greater the results.

Ho'oponopono is remarkable healing work for known generational trauma, as well as unconscious soul wounds—for past, present, and future familial dysfunction. Past trauma is stored on a preprogrammed cellular level in our bodies, so deep it seems like we can never reach it, yet it continues to agitate our nervous system, dictating poor behavior and choices we make now. We unconsciously pass the pain on to others, mainly our children. Imago therapists call this the "legacy of wounding." In *Getting the Love You Want*, Hendrix and

LaKelly Hunt describe it as passing on trauma without knowledge or consent, recreating emotional abandonment. Healing generational traumatic dysfunction (as well as nontraumatic dysfunction) with this mantra can halt the recreation of painful wounds caused by emotional abandonment. Self-compassion and self-forgiveness free our souls of the hefty weight we carry, and we stop passing it on.

You are connected to all the souls in your family tree and can bring healing through compassion and forgiveness to every family member you've ever had or will have. Cleaning known or unknown hurt is a path to high-frequency freedom for you, for the generations that came before you, and for the ones to follow. Requesting forgiveness without knowing why you did what you did is a powerful tool for this type of healing. When you trust the universe to know exactly what you need to heal, you are no longer responsible for figuring out the root cause of the pain.

This offering is the jewel in the crown of trust.

As pain spreads like a fast-growing, invasive vine, healing has the same widespread ripple effect. Once you spark the vibrations of health and wellness, they will reach farther and wider than your temporal brain can fathom, and with speed. Ho'oponopono is the invitation for these good vibrations of exceptional healing.

Adding self-compassion and forgiveness to humility and understanding, we now have a comprehensive blueprint for releasing pain and for healing.

I heard about this ancient wisdom at the same time Jim reintroduced me to Imago Theory, while I was learning about emotional abandonment in therapy as well as in a twelve-step program (one I stumbled upon thinking I was attending a meeting only to treat my alcoholism). I was exposed to the effects of generational dysfunction through four unrelated sources while attempting to figure out why I felt disconnected from my husband. This had to be more than coincidence. Something, or someone, was trying to get my attention.

And they had it!

18

THE PLACE OF ONENESS

My success is not measured by this piece of writing or the letters after my name. My success lies in how safe I feel in my own presence and how far I extend that comfort to others. The importance of my legacy will be directly proportional to how well people feel when they are around me. It will be measured by my willingness to jump into bewildering moments of life—the run-of-the-mill kind and the ones that slaughter me.

Do I jump in ready to welcome myself and others in a nonjudgmental, warm way, with an open heart and an open mind? Do I join people in their experience so they feel seen, heard, and loved or am I drifting off, thinking about what I am getting out of the exchange? Am I focused on how they make me feel instead of how I make them feel? Can I put my emotional needs aside and step into someone's essence to be fully present with them?

Do I shut down in self-protection or grow my spirit in connected love?

Empathy implies I understand your pain, which is beautiful, but I do not think this definition is broad enough to explain the range of connection I am speaking about. I want to go further in to feel *your* pain, not identifying the feelings as they relate to me separately. I want to be down in the trenches with you, feeling your struggle as you feel it. I want to get as close as I can, trusting I will emerge from your darkness, which is now more of a dusk since sharing lightens the load, with my own self intact and with you feeling as though you are not alone. It's impossible to feel your pain exactly as you do, but I can come extraordinarily close by focusing on your sorrow and forgetting about me for the time being.

I spent hours exploring this space during the height of my 2020 despair over the extreme division of humanity. The differing opinions about how to handle the pandemic as well as tension over racial inequality and the United States presidential election cast me into profound feeling and thought. I asked my Higher Self in my daily meditation sessions: *Can I step out of my humanness, my ego, and meet you vulnerably in a place where I am safe to feel your pain and your fear? Can I trust I will not leave a part of my soul in that vast, discomforting space? Can I be compassionate when I cannot understand why you feel the way you do or when I am afraid to feel what you feel because it seems dark to me? Will the self-centered, egoic lies abound to keep me separate and safe in my armor?*

I was scared to do this work and shed a couple of tears before going into the pain of others, but I knew I had to if I wanted to be an agent of change. I considered the way I see the world is not how everyone sees the world and my ideas and beliefs are not right for all. I considered ideas and beliefs contrary to mine. (I understood some of them well after hard conversations with friends and family who felt the opposite way about current events than I did.) I tried to feel what they felt and to enter their pain. Comparing their fear to my fear, I saw how we feared the same thing, and how we wanted the same thing—health, happiness, and peace. We just had different ideas about how to get there.

Gathering the fear energy in the meditation cave, I acknowledged our disconnection and entered it. Leaning into this painful energy, I asked my High Guides how we, as a society, can release the grip that fear had on the planet. They told me to invite the healing energy of love and compassion in and to allow that healing energy to become stronger than the fear. Staring at a robust flame of a candle, I pictured it burn away the fear and saw light enter our dark world. I watched the light engulf the fear totally and completely. I lit sage, felt healing take place, and cried. I practiced Metta meditation, fired up the Ring of Love, and reached for the hands of those with conflicting beliefs. My tears of pain turned to tears of hope, relief, and joy.

I sat in the healing light for a while (until a couple of small children came looking for their mommy) and asked for gratitude to enter my heart. I felt grateful for the world's tribulation because I knew this was the beginning of a shift, an uprooting of old belief systems. I felt the world's growing pains as we forge new ideologies, behaviors, and patterns.

Tightly packed dirt excavated, picked up, and thrown in the air like confetti entered my vision. Some people tried to gather the unruly specks of dirt together in an attempt to pack it back down into a controlled, stable pile of predictability. Other people watched from the sidelines, calmly and peacefully. They knew the dirt had to be uprooted and tossed around for it to land in a new landscape, a better design, and they did not have to enter the frenzy because life was happening in divine order. I met all who were present in that image where they were and sent them love.

I invited my children into the cave, we blew out the candle, and then went upstairs and made chocolate chip pancakes for breakfast.

The world was going to be okay.

I found the courage to meet the people of the world in their pain by meeting Jim in his during our Imago Therapy work. We were in a much better place in 2020, but I wanted more. I needed more and was willing to meet him in this vulnerable space. This meant I had to look honestly at my calloused heart and find a way to soften it.

Desperate, with a yearning to be all in with Jim, I met him ready to share from my soul with no expectations. I was so beaten down by grief at this point that nothing either of us shared could hurt me anymore than I had already been hurt. Going in with no expectation, I thought less about what I needed to get out of the conversation and more about what Jim needed to share with me. I wanted to make him feel understood and loved and to extend comfort to him. He expressed he wanted to do the same for me.

We entered each other's vulnerability with guards lowered. Feeling at ease by the other's defenseless presence, our expressions indicated we would receive one another with a compassionate heart.

We felt safe to open up, share from our souls, and listen to each other's words. Love and forgiveness began to flow mutually as we shared our vulnerable truths. Unencumbered by the shields we wore to protect ourselves, we saw and heard each other, learning what the other needed and wasn't getting: attention, affection, quality time, patience, appreciation, understanding, and compassion. Most of our unfilled longings were the same, and we found common ground in this shared pain. It created intimacy. I told Jim about my fear of him dying, and we further explored the source of The Great Myth.

Think of this sharing like a Venn diagram, two circles overlapping in the center. The section on the left is my vulnerability, the one on the right is yours, and the sacred place in the center is where we meet. My essence moves freely between the sections, visiting each one as I transition safely between them. One section is not entered into at the full expense of any other; maintaining the three sections (me, you, and us) as separate entities is crucial to the process. However, I feel safe enough to enter your circle for a while, allow my ego to dissipate, and meet you wholly in your suffering, pain, and fear. I'm not afraid to meet you there because I trust I will not become enmeshed and lose myself. I do not need to give away my whole self to wholeheartedly feel you.

When I trust myself to emerge from your circle and you trust that I feel you, we safely venture into the center, joining our separate compassionate selves as one. Blending the soul of the universe residing within our individual souls, we meet in the place of oneness. United in a togetherness that cannot be separated by the classification of you and me, we are one, seeing each other in the light of shared suffering. This is the home of true connected compassion, of namaste. It's where we feel safe to give the best of ourselves.

There were moments in the place of oneness with Jim when the fear became overwhelming and my defenses went up. Unable to be my best self, I backslid into emotional comfort at the expense of meeting Jim in his pain. It was okay. I practiced self-compassion, allowed myself to be human, and tried again.

Backsliding is essential to keep moving forward. The fear of not completing my mission—to love honestly with rawness and vulnerability and to strive for this without conditions—motivates me to try again, and with more oomph. So I don the boxing gloves, meet fear in the parking lot, and go for another round.

I don't leave the ring until I feel safe in my emotions, safe enough to love.

Setting up an environment for the transfer of peaceful words and notions is the entryway to purposeful communication, understanding, and connection you can trust. And it starts with you. Reaching out first, with sincerity, prepares the ground for others to feel safe to open up about their pain. What a blessing for the person you are involved with! To have someone in her or his life who is willing to set up this space is a blessing indeed.

You may wish to design the space warmly, but frustration and anger may be the first emotions on the scene. They are often required for the process. Anxiety-producing at the onset, these stressful emotions must be expressed or your partner may be left feeling misunderstood. Dark emotions will most likely transform into pleasant ones and should be honored for what they are before mutating into calm, compassionate vulnerability, an indispensable element of this process.

The way to meet others in their vulnerability is to meet your own. I cannot meet you unguarded if I am uncomfortable unguarded, and what keeps me uncomfortable in vulnerability is fear of what I will find when I look at my pain. Calling forth bravery, I remember the goal: to create a safe space for you to express yourself honestly and authentically so a trustworthy, healing connection can be made. This requires acceptance.

Allowing each other to be exactly who we are in that moment is the base from which feelings like vulnerability, compassion, and selflessness rise. Selflessness, in this case, means we do not try to make people feel better when they are upset. We accept them where they are, respecting how they feel no matter what it churns up in us.

We like to talk people out of pain, disguising it as care and concern when, in actuality, we are trying to avoid our own uneasy feelings to protect ourselves. Fear of being unable to handle anxiety overwhelms. It's why I tell my kids they are okay when they fall from the monkey bars and cry. They aren't okay, but instead of trying to convince them they are (to lessen my feelings of powerlessness), I've learned to meet them in their tears so they feel seen and loved. This ends their pain faster than when I minimize how they feel because I am looking to relieve my own discomfort. You do not have to make anyone's pain go away. Most people prefer for you to not make it go away. They just want someone to assure them they are not alone.

The principles you read about—compassion, selflessness, and open-heartedness, among others—will give you the best chance of creating a healing place of oneness. And now that you know how to step into these principles with grace, courage, and resilience, you are ready. If the person is hesitant to meet you there, do it anyway. Tell that person how you feel with an unguarded heart. If you feel disappointed, try not to be. Creating this space allows for both of you to grow, but like Compassion Forgiveness and Esteemable Boundaries, the healing is for you. You receive so much from the encounter: the gift of feeling love grows inside you because you acted in love. You became love and compassion. You also possessed courage and dignity, all worthy virtues. Your self-worth will multiply step by step as you walk away knowing you showed up as an ally to yourself, loyal to your emotional integrity and personal growth.

So, will you initiate healing? Will you set up the place of oneness and welcome whatever emotions may appear? Can you push past your comfort zone and go as far as your soul and this world need you to go? Will you be all in?

I hope your answer is yes because the universe needs to feel your light.

19

THE TRUST
MUSCLE

F ear of loss comes up while watching sad movies, when someone close to me gets a grim medical diagnosis, when my
daughter graduates from kindergarten, or when singing happy
birthday to my dog. It happens in times of celebration and times of
sorrow. My mind advances to future grief, often fast-forwarding to
the worst-case scenario, and it's a struggle to keep an open heart of
trust. In fear, I pull away.

It's about mindfulness in these moments. I'm mindfully aware
when self-reliance becomes my copilot and I'm flying alone, me and
my faithful friend fear. I must seek balance to escort myself back to
emotional security, trusting I will land there safely.

Stepping into the fear, I challenge myself to move toward safety
and comfort. Toggling and enduring the space between, I magnify

the fear like a virus under a microscope, uncovering its origin and inspecting it for as long as my anxiety will allow. Observing patterns, or triggers of grief, I seize the opportunity to grow by sitting in the discomfort. This is an exercise in training my capacity for emotional intimacy within myself.

As with all growth, I must practice feeling comfortable in emotional intimacy if I want to become good at it. If I want to be a good dancer, I have to put on my jazz shoes and get in the studio. If I want to be a good tennis player, I have to spend time on the court. If I want to be comfortable in emotional intimacy, I must practice feeling safe and secure when I feel unsafe and insecure. As I sit in this uncomfortable place, I strengthen the trust muscle by practicing being okay. I begin to see that right here, right now, in this moment, I am okay. I practice living for today and just for today.

Safe in emotional intimacy, I start to feel emotionally secure. Comfortable there, I consider how I might handle the worst-case scenario, should it come to pass. I place myself smack in the middle of that scenario. It's usually not as scary as my brain wants me to believe it to be. I begin to realize I can and will handle whatever emotional demands that situation may bring, as I've handled every affliction to date. My trust muscle grows as I review painful past experiences and acknowledge I have not only made it through successfully, but each one has resulted in a stronger, wiser Amanda.

This is an example of reframing, another useful tool to practice being okay. Reframing my thoughts from *It's dangerous to love; I won't survive the loss,* to *It's safe to love; I will always be okay,* I use the fear as a tool to shore up my trust in self. I alter my perspective and learn to function from a place of emotional security instead of emotional abandonment. I go into the moment with an open, loving heart instead of running away. Where I used to be consumed with fear of loss, I now focus on my ability to make it through the pain. I watch the space mutate from dangerous to safe, from fear of loss to trust in self.

When fear doesn't allow me to reframe my thoughts, I interval train my bandwidth for emotional intimacy. Two steps forward into scary feelings and one step back into comfort gets me there. Likewise, I can take one step forward and linger there for as long as I need to, then take another tentative step forward. I gain traction, then momentum, and before I know it I am safe in emotional intimacy.

I make the effort to connect with precious moments and people because they will evaporate someday. I'm unwilling to let them pass in vain. Communing with source energy, nurturing my relationship with it, and trusting it to lead me successfully through future pain is my path to safe connection with self and others. I feel confident to show up emotionally and intelligently, secure knowing my faculties will arise when needed and the direction I'm meant to move in will be revealed. In essence, I'm okay knowing the fluffy, white clouds may turn dark. I no longer fear the storm.

When I can't do that, I do what my down-to-earth cousin told me to do as she coached me through the initial shock of Jeremy's death. As I paced around the dining room table, my mind searching its defenses for protection, she softly voiced, "Just keep breathing."

Humans are fallible. They let us down; they die. Knowing people, places, and situations are fleeting, as the reality of impermanence affirms, who and what can you unreservedly trust to never let you down? The who is you and your Higher Power who dwells inside; the what is your worth.

Are you ready for that level of commitment? Do you trust yourself and the Universal Spirit within to show up for you unconditionally? Will you be there for yourself with comfort and consolation through the most grueling loss and pain, through the joy and the jubilation? Do you trust yourself to no longer abandon the wise soul that is uniquely you with the same confidence you have in the sun to rise each day? Is your trust muscle weak or strong?

I've spent many years in active self-betrayal. Feeling unsafe and distrusting people and the world around me, I was forced to create a shape-shift sort of identity: the chameleon. Fear kept me from showing up consistently with true colors. The pressure to meet the demands of my environment (to survive in an unsafe world) dictated which Amanda appeared. How could I trust myself to be me if I didn't know who I was? Misaligned with my True Self, I exited most social encounters defeated and anxious. Severely disconnected from my truth, I self-abandoned. How could I trust myself to protect the child, young adult, and woman I was supposed to be taking care of while unacquainted with her?

It took sixteen years of spiritual seeking to reach a point when I can say I trust myself, my spirit, and my soul to never let me down, and I can do so without shame of feeling good. I no longer abandon myself. Well, to be honest, I no longer abandon myself as often as I used to. Where I used to spend a week mulling over a situation or a conversation, I am now able to put these events into perspective quickly, withdrawing myself as the main culprit. Upon occasion,

I flirt with self-sabotage, self-criticism, and self-doubt, and when those feelings rear their ugly heads, I see them, give them a gentle hug, and send them on their merry little way.

Doing the work to love the woman I am today grants me safety to go anywhere, at any time, resolute in my character. I am me regardless of the people I'm with or the setting I am in. When others feel this energy, it's easier for them to meet me there and make a trustworthy connection. A connection doesn't always happen, and it's not my responsibility to make it happen. My job is to provide an opening by showing up in love and remaining unchanged by others. Staying true to myself when a healthy, honest connection is present, I am safe to engage. If the person does not respond, I am safe to back away and let go without feeling abandoned.

Tune in to how you feel when around potential friends. Trust your gut. It never lies. A few questions to ponder when selecting your crew are: When you drive away from someone, do you crank up your favorite song and sing the whole way home? Whom would you choose to be in the passenger seat next to you? Who feels like the sun's rays beaming on your face, warming you up?

Stay close to the people with whom you feel grounded. Those are your people, and it's not by chance you recognize their energy. Your instincts are speaking; you know each other on a soul level or remember each other from a past life. There is a reason you've been brought together, a lesson to be learned. If they leave, trust the lesson has been learned and let them go placidly, like a bird flying south at the first hint of snow. If the lesson requires a sequel, they will come back, like the hummingbird in spring.

When you trust this abundant, all-knowing, whirling totality to work its magic, it's hard to feel abandoned. Besides, you are never abandoned when you have yourself.

On a warm August afternoon during the pandemic, I decided who I wanted in my life and in what capacity. I placed these people in my trust tree, a metaphor I've heard before, but now internalized and made my own.

Each person in my trust tree does not occupy the same branch or carry the same weight. They all have their own places and serve specific needs. Some people are located on the outermost leaves, threatening to fall if the wind gusts too hard. Others are on twig-like limbs, stretching far from the trunk. Some are on thick branches near the core; other people are located in the sturdy trunk. Then there are those cozied up in the nest. The closer to the nest, the more I trust them and the more we experience the interchange of love.

Loved ones in my nest are my safest place. They oxygenate my being and make me feel alive. The further they are from my nest, the less I trust people with my innermost thoughts and feelings, but they serve a purpose and deserve respect. I do not go deep with every person in my tree. Rather, I try to extend a warm heart, an open mind, and a spirit of loving-kindness to all.

The year 2020 blared the horn on people's personal ideologies with shocking realism, causing me to experience numerous jaw-to-the-floor moments of total disbelief. There were times I had to search hard for the goodness in people, but I always found it. I found their hearts. Again, no matter how people present, their true heart is love.

That I trust. Even so, some people organically slid down the branches of my trust tree; they are still in my tree but live in a place further from the nest. Other people fell out, and some came in closer. You do not have to kick people out of your tree, nor do they need to be in your nest. They can hang out wherever you feel comfortable letting them hang out.

Unsure about how to address a friend about our waning friendship after the pandemic, I got quiet, listened for guidance, and sought courage to ask what was going on. We talked honestly about the root of the problem—a situation I was unaware of. I apologized for hurting her feelings, and she apologized for waiting to talk about it with me. We realized we missed each other deeply. The pain of our separation exceeded the pain of our misunderstanding, and we decided to get together.

Another time, I addressed an estranged friend, and she was not interested in coming in closer. I respected her desire for space and mourned the loss of what was once a close friendship. On another occasion, the person who pulled away did not return my calls and texts. I must accept where people are in their lives and their lack of desire to remain close to me. It's okay. I still love them.

You may wonder how the people dangling from the leaves of your tree are trustworthy. How can you trust them to be dependable when their existence is mercurial? You trust them because your terms of endearment are not in direct proportion to what they are able to return. You trust them, to varying degrees, not because of who they are but because of who you are; your character and self-worth are unconditional. Fear of loss does not control you when people fall away to become compost for next year's regrowth or decide to never bless your tree again. They do not take a big piece of you with them because they do not define you.

No one defines you when your universal self is intact.

Can you allow certain people, or groups of people, to flow in and out of your sensitive heart space without demanding they stay there? More painfully, can you accept when someone does not want to be close with you when you desperately want them to be? This is harder than allowing people to flow in and out, but it need not worry you because you are learning to trust that you will be okay when loss presents. You are strengthening the trust muscle.

I hate to be the bearer of bad news, but you won't jibe with everyone. Fret not; it's by design. Feelings of aversion toward some-one indicates your energy is exhausted—something is not right. You're not meshing, and that's okay. You don't have to force what is not meant to be. We spend valuable time trying to force the hand of connection when it may be time to let go and free up space for someone else to flow in.

Similarly, you will find people who you easily connect with but who will not allow the connection to reach them. They can feel the prospect of a heartfelt partnership, but they will not, or cannot, reciprocate. Comfortably idling in an outer layer of your trust tree, they are uninterested in moving closer. Can you accept these people into your tree and not pressure them to come near the nest? Do you trust the level of intimacy in these relationships as part of the grand scheme?

Trust the differing levels of connection inherent in the relationships in your life. There are those who are not supposed to be in your inner circle and those who indubitably are. Some people may remain on a twig-like limb forever, never making it into your nest; others will never leave the nest, and some will not make it into your tree. Each soul is where it is meant to be when it is meant to be.

Respecting someone's wishes, direct or indirect, to back off is at the heart of selflessness, grace, and trust. Releasing the need for someone to be something they are not capable of or do not want to be is compassion in its Sunday best, for you and for that person.

20

TRUST YOUR PROCESS

L et all you encounter cascade like a waterfall landing in a pool of faith. Continuously circulating, it flows wherever it's supposed to. It does not resist its migration to and fro, near or far; it goes with the wind. When you trust your intuition to communicate the direction you are meant to flow next, and you know higher forces are devoted to guiding you, you can sail through life with ease. You can trust your process.

Feel into your intuition when you are going against your tide. Get familiar with it. Trust it, for it is accurate and reliable. Learn what if feels like to be pushed toward or away from people, places, possessions, or ideas. Check in with your Higher Power and your Higher Self and get honest. Why are you moving toward or away from something?

Contemplative meditation is the perfect type of meditation for this check-in process. We can do it anytime we're faced with a situation requiring an immediate response. It's an ongoing consciousness as we move about our day—brushing teeth, washing dishes, driving in the car. It is not reserved for an appointed time, in an appointed place, so we can be busy living and tuned in at the same time. This meditation does not require candles, incense, or literature. (No meditation does.) All you need is an awareness of a high-frequency force field around you, which you can tap into at will, and an open mind to seek direction based in truth.

A cousin to mindfulness, my moving practice of contemplative meditation looks like this: I ask a question. When I feel something like an answer, I contemplate if it's my self-will/personal desire or my Higher Self/Spirit. I feel deeper into the message I'm receiving. If it does not feel in alignment with my soul, I discard it and try again. I wait, with the intention to understand. Once my soul and thoughts recognize each other as old friends, I travel deeper into the answer, seeking more direction. As I continue to discern if my intuition is coming from my inner guides or my own mind, I ask additional questions and listen for more messages while gaining insight. If nothing else comes, I accept I'm not supposed to have access to the information at that moment. This process takes a short amount of time, and I do not need to be sitting in lotus position to engage in it.

It's harder to tap in when driving Johnny to soccer practice, at the drive-through window, or in the check-out line because we are preoccupied and not as receptive, but the energy is present. It's the same energy we feel when holding a child on our lap in silence; when connecting with nature, animals, and art; and when we hug our friends. It's the elusive but nonetheless real feeling that exists in the space between you, me, and all that is. Intangible, yet perceivable, it's the essence of love and truth. I deliberately manifest this energy in everyday scenarios—at the drive-through window and in the check-out line—and the more I practice stepping into this space, the quicker the messages arrive.

Upon receiving a message, feel into it for a confirmation or for a, "Nah, that's not it." Don't talk yourself into the "Nah," because you don't like the answer you get. Ask for clarification, then clarify some more, especially when the decision impacts others. It takes a bit of extra effort but is worth the push if you receive beneficial guidance for you and others.

Do not take action until the confirmation is clear. Listen hard, and you will be advised whether you should act sooner, later, or not at all. When it's time to take action, divinity will show itself with persistent urges. An insistent tug is the universe telling you the motion is ready for action; it's scheduled, and it's time to pull the trigger. Divinity will also let you know if you should wait. While you wait, you don't have to do much. Just settle into the box seats of the greatest show on Earth: your life.

The rest will take care of itself.

When you trust your soul's process, the universe will deliver, but you must be alert. Make sense of what you stumble upon. Observe what is placed before you for there are no mistakes, no haphazardly placed elements. Use what's in front of you to your advantage. These personal offerings are there to help you, and how you elucidate and allow them to guide you is up to you.

There is no such thing as chance when it comes to signs from the universe. Wherever your attention is pulled to—a song on the radio, the phone number on the side of a taxicab, the words on a billboard, the drawing your child left on the counter, a songbird chirping in a tree—these are the messengers. You only need to be receptive to them. When they appear, check in with your soul for connection and believe the messages are for you. Appearing random, they are not.

Synchronicity is a strong conveyor of messages, and it's everywhere.

I am astounded how the number seventy-two appears in my life in not-so-subtle ways. It's part of my hometown zip code, my social security number, the address of Grandma Tessie's Queens apartment (Mom's childhood home), and my first license plate. Seven and two are next to each other in the dates of prominent moments in my life: my first date with Jim, the day we became domestic partners, my last drinking binge. July 20 (7/20) was the due date of the six-week-old embryo we lost before our first daughter was born. My paternal grandmother died in 1972. Seven and two are the first two numbers in the address of the church Jim and I were married in. The list goes on …

Coincidence as an explanation for seemingly unconnected events in life is full of holes. It is the guise of divine timing, the universe's great attempt to transmit messages, and it never disappoints. Signs come to me in rapid succession too often to be happenstance, like when I think of my niece, Jeremy's beautiful gift to the world, and I check Pearl Jam Radio on SiriusXM and "Daughter" is playing. Sometimes I doubt signs he is with me, then I round the corner to see a red Jeep, a symbol for my brother. As I'm still questioning the legitimacy of my thoughts, a crow flies overhead and is over my house when I pull into the driveway. The crow is the ultimate sign of Jeremy's presence. You decide if that's coincidence.

Technology is hard at work conveying messages too. Mind what pops up in your social media feed. My Instagram speaks to me. It's as if it reads my mind. (I hope we are not there yet.) Kicking an idea around my head, I open the app and what I was thinking about appears like an implicit affirmation gifted from the social media gods.

This phenomenon occurs in your life too. Noticing one occurrence opens the door. One awareness leads to the next and to the next until you cannot deny the universe is speaking to you.

The more you see, the more you can see.

You set off a snowball effect of thoughts and events once you find the synchronicity. This exchange of energy is known as co-creation, and for it to manifest you must have a personal relationship with the universe. You must spend time with it. Learn how it communicates personally with you and how you best receive, as we all receive differently. My signs are tailored for me. Yours are tailored for you. Ask the universe to help you see the signs and understand what they mean. Maintain your thought pattern or readjust it based on the feedback you get—mental feedback as well as material. If stuck, seek the messages another way; visit a forest or the ocean, go for a run, listen to music, or write.

Resounding into the universe, your thoughts will return to you as inspiration from your Higher Self, but only if you believe they will, and the volley of thoughts and inspiration will continue for as long as you want them to. Some inspiration will push you out of your comfort zone. It will feel demanding and hard to execute, and it may be, but keep at it. The truth is that success is already yours, waiting to be realized.

On the other hand, if you don't believe you will receive inspiration, you won't. Sometimes the limiting belief systems we carry are hidden and difficult to recognize. We don't know we are closed off. We think we are open, when really we are afraid or doubtful. Prayer and meditation can unlock your subconscious mind to present the truth: Your potential to receive inspiration is as boundless as you believe it to be, and your potential to believe is as great as your desire to believe. After belief comes trust.

Trust, then receive. That's the key, the code. You program the universe with what to provide you. Showing up in the powerful energy of trust tells the universe you are ready to receive. The messages will not come if you do not trust in your power to receive, and you cannot lie to the universe. It knows.

Will you let the postcards from the unknown reach you, filled with the goodness synchronicity is constantly trying to deliver? Or will you shut down your mind's eye without giving it a chance to connect with you?

Trust in your inherent connection to source and what it is trying to teach you. You will be amazed rather quickly.

21
ROOT & RELEASE

My meditation practice has evolved over the years. The basic tenets of light and love are the same as in my early days of meditating, but now I guide the sessions less as I feel safer to transit closer to my truth. Releasing control, I ask my Higher Power to fix my eyes and my ears so I may see and hear the world as it is, not as I want it to be. I used to pray for outcomes; now I pray for willingness to accept life as it happens, whether it's what I want or not.

When I surrender to Spirit, my personal wishes fade as I allow the energy to do with me what it must. I ask God and my Master Guides to tune my antennae to the channel of peace, to open me up for pure love to move in and through me. I'm pulled toward different readings, oracle cards, essential oils, crystals, and stones, which aid in opening the main line.

To access a conduit for my Higher Power, I open the main line of energy through a grounding technique. With feet firmly planted on the floor, tree roots begin to grow from my soles, extending down into the earth. I start to breathe deeply. With each breath in, I inhale all I am and all we are: our calm, excitement, confusion, failings, resilience, sadness, and joy. With each breath out, the roots burrow into the solid floor below me, taking all we are with it. Descending through the rug, the wood, the concrete foundation, and the mineral-rich, rocky soil, my roots continue to travel down through the layers of the earth until they reach the core, where all we are is healed by the high-frequency energy of the planet.

I am now connected to the entire world.

I continue to breathe. My trunk becomes taller and stronger with each breath in, and my roots reach deeper with each breath out. I am grounded into the core of the material plane while my spirit unites with cosmic consciousness. Sturdy, yet able to sway in the winds of harmony and healing, the crown of my tree mingles with the crowns of the trees around me as we supply oxygen to the world. One with the flow, a tree among many, a tree among all humans, together we give life to our beautiful planet. Safe and protected in our forest of life, breathing in unison, our energy merges with the rhythm of the universal soul. Hearts beat as one; minds connect in higher knowing. Direction for who my Higher Power wants me to be and what it wants me to do drops smoothly into my being.

I pray for courage to serve creation well today, tomorrow, and hereafter.

I stay there for a while, soaking in this collective cosmic energy before moving on to clear my chakras. Chakras are energy centers in and around our bodies that control the flow of good, healing energy (the same energy, or chi, found in EFT tapping). At times, chakras become blocked, usually with fear and other negative emotions that need to be cleared. There are seven chakras located along the length of the spine, and five more outside the body. I work with the primary seven within my body.

As an empath, I easily absorb energy that does not belong to me. Cleansing chakras clears the energy and helps me receive pure direction for my highest good and for the highest good of those around me. Before starting chakra work, I visualize myself encased in a six-pointed, eight-faced octahedron of high-frequency energy. Placing a starlit point two feet in front of me, two feet behind me, two feet to my right, and to my left, above, and below, I am encased in a sacred geometry of high vibration. Safe and protected from energies that try to invade my aura, I'm transported to an astral plane of love and light, and the chakra work begins.

Beginning in the base of the spine at the root chakra, which grounds and connects me to the universe as well as our physical existence, I focus on the tree roots extending from the bottom of my feet into the core of the earth. Maintaining this visual, I reinforce my connection with all that is, producing a feeling of safety in both the universal and physical atmospheres of life. Trust in the energy-clearing process is established here, and the color is red.

The chakra above the root, a few inches below the belly button, is the sacral chakra. The color is orange. This is the creativity center. Located in the sacred reproductive organ area of the body, it's where we bring light into the world through creative endeavors. This light is similar to the light birthed when we enter the world, super-charged with power to achieve anything. Cleansing and clearing this energy field fires my imagination and sparks my artistry. Inspired to bring healing light into the world, I receive messages to create in ways I was previously closed off to.

The next chakra is the solar plexus. It's yellow and located a few inches above the belly button. Confidence, self-esteem, personal power, and physical health live here. It's interesting that the chakra responsible for overall health is located in the abdomen, as science is discovering disease stems from microbiota in the gut. Stepping into personal power by clearing the solar plexus may be directly linked to lowering risk for disease.

Above the solar plexus is the heart chakra. For me, this is the epicenter of love and healing where I transmute fear into trust, hurt into healing. The rusty gates of my heart reside here, and the color is green. The Metta part of my meditation begins. I watch the gates open to welcome opalescent green light, feel it heal me, then send it out: receive, heal, send, receive, heal, send. The energy becomes activated when shifted from fear and hurt to trust and healing and expands exponentially during this sacred cycle.

Developing and nurturing this part of the process is the fast track to a congruous planet. Peaceful energy resonates in the ethereal and ricochets, promoting positivity, goodwill, and a desire to compassionately connect as one. Doing this in unison with others holds even more power. When a large group of people focuses on being love simultaneously, it vigorously upgrades participants' internal frequency. As our individual frequency upgrades, the frequency of the universe rises. When the frequency of the universe rises, flowers bloom, grass grows, and dolphins breach the surface of the ocean. Earth flourishes, and when Earth flourishes, we flourish.

The heart chakra is the place of oneness, the home of namaste (think Venn diagram), where my soul sees and honors yours and I see and honor my own soul. When I see and honor my soul, I can't help but feel love for myself. Feeling love for myself, I feel love for you. This is what my spiritual practice boils down to. Healing me heals you, and when we heal collectively, we heal the world.

Above the heart is the throat chakra. It is sky blue and controls communication. Once the heart is open to limitless, collective love, then we use words to express that love. Words hold great power to hurt, heal, and manifest; they create a reality of emotion, thought, attitude, and action that affects not only our own lives but the whole world. Respecting the power I have to bring harmony, healing, and creativity to the planet, I must make sure I'm choosing words responsibly and thoughtfully, with kindness and compassion. We all have this obligation when speaking with anyone, at any time, including with ourselves and the spirit world. Clearing the throat chakra puts us in a better position to do this.

Next is the third eye chakra, our soul sight. This is our spiritual wisdom, and the color is indigo. It's located in the middle of the forehead. When clear, this chakra helps us see, hear, feel, and know things beyond our physical senses. Opening an avenue of higher consciousness, extrasensory perception, and intuition, our third eye connects with our ego to help us glean a clear image of what's going on in and around us. As we feel and know things on a higher plane, the ego shrinks. Humbled and open, we are free to receive transmissions from the universe.

The seventh chakra is our crown chakra and is found at the top of our heads. The color is violet or white. This is where we transcend human constrictions on our knowing and become one with the universe. Enlightened in connection with lifeforce energy and our High Guides, a change in perception occurs. No longer limited by physicality, we experience the power of infinite thought.

Visuals are useful to initiate the flow of energy to and through our centers and are especially useful for opening the crown chakra. I imagine a beam of light enters my body through the top of my head, and I watch it travel to the end of my toes. Others welcome this light through a crown of flowers. Filled with a warm tower of light, powerful spirit energy moves in and through me. A slight buzzing sensation indicates spirit and body are united as one. I'm more open and intuitive in this encasement, even if for only three minutes, than I am the rest of the day.

Enveloped in light, I begin sending restorative energy to clean and clear each chakra from the root to the crown. With one chakra lit, I move upward toward the next, loosening the sludge that clogs my free-flowing energy. When all seven energy centers are spinning freely and shining brightly (a phrase common to the chakra-clearing processes), I am an incandescent, brilliant rainbow aware of and sensitive to inconspicuous thoughts and feelings—ones that serve me and the world around me, and ones that do not. I give power to the ones that do and release the ones that do not through the tree roots extending from the bottom of my feet into the core of the Earth. I ask my High Guides to take the negative energy, and I begin to feel lighter almost immediately. I am left peaceful, positive, and safe in my being.

After my chakras are cleansed and cleared, I practice yoga nidra, or conscious relaxation. Yoga nidra is a meditation of consciously relaxing each part of the body, aware of its state as you move from one area to the next. Dopamine levels, as well as theta brain waves, increase to give me an easy, mellow feeling. This helps me relax even more and heightens my sense of what's going on inside. Each piece of anatomy is directly linked to a certain emotion or knowing, and pain or movement is the body's way of getting our attention. It's easier to identify these messages while in the conscious state of yoga nidra.

My body speaks through pulsing, tingling, ringing, and throbbing. When my hands buzz, it's time to get creative. When my lower back stings, I ask what emotional stress needs to be released. Pressure on my shoulders means I'm not alone; a higher force is present. Ringing in the ears indicates I am in tune; the message is coming from spirit and is true. I am still connected to crown energy during this process. Once I break communion with crown energy, the healing benefits of this work remain, as do fragments of the knowing, but the vibrating sensation of universal connection recedes.

I tune in to my body throughout the day as it holds healing solutions. Reactions from childhood persist, and noticing and releasing them is good for my physical and emotional health. I stuttered, bit my nails, and was constipated as a child. (Anxious much?) Hiding behind the floor-length drapes in the living room, I held in bowel movements. Suffering from fear and anxiety, this was one of my coping skills, my attempt to control whatever I could, which as a child was not much: not my parents arguing, my distress around men, or my low self-worth. I still find myself clenching "down there" at times (I'm an expert Kegel-er) and consciously work to release that tension when noticed. Letting go tells my brain I am physically safe, and I am able to release control in other areas of my life. Physical safety translates to emotional safety.

Surrender to your unconscious bodily responses. Ask to be made aware. Resisting will make the anxiety or tension grow. Once you identify a blockage, ask yourself what is creating the response. Tap into emotional difficulty and connect the dots to see how your past experiences manifest in the present. Upon revelation, allow yourself to release the anxiety. Mindfully move it, clear it, and then welcome tranquility.

Mindfully sending energy to areas of the body and having the power to move it is legit. The miracle of childbirth proves this. During labor with my first child, epidural administered and numb, I was told to push.

I questioned, "How am I supposed to push when I can't feel anything?"

The nurse urged, "Focus and push."

I concentrated on my abdominal and pelvic muscles. I sent extrasensory power to my little girl's entrance into the world, and out she came. If we can do that, then mindfully moving and sending healing energy to ourselves and to others is not a far-fetched proposition.

It's real if you believe it.

22
ALLOW

Allowing is the process of letting conscious and unconscious thoughts, feelings, and emotions flow effortlessly in and through us. It's a fluid art form that takes solid shape with regular practice. When we allow, we welcome goodness for all. The universe knows we are ready to respond to its gentle, steady, loving whisper, and life manifests in ways that serve our individual needs and humanity best.

Allowing is an ever-widening, cyclical circle of high-frequency energy. As you allow yourself to become a conduit—a vessel for receiving and emitting love—you are blessed with more high-frequency energy, more love, and more momentum, which motivates you to continue allowing. Good things start to roll into your head, heart, and life. They trickle in slowly at first, but with practice they start to arrive with precision and speed, like a bowling ball that hits a few pins, then rolls a spare, then a strike. The higher vibrations you put out, the more pins you hit, and the better life gets.

The action you take builds the momentum, kick-starting the process of allowing. After the action, let go. Trust all will be well once you let go, independent of the outcome. Trust *you* will be well because your safety and security no longer depend on outcomes. It feels scary until you try it and find that allowing yields better results than running on self-will. When you move out of the way with a sense of security, your energy permits the innate beauty of the universe to cast its blessings upon you. Something bigger than you calls the shots, and those shots are often much better than you could have executed yourself.

Our society has a tendency to view alone time as dangerous isolation. This is not true. You don't always have to be in the middle of the herd. You are allowed to be by yourself to bounce back from the hustle and bustle of the material world, to come back to your authentic center.

Allow alone time.

Alone time, or finding solace in solitude, is essential to reveal your true essence hidden under man-made constructs, to find safety in a world that often feels unsafe. We use the word "rejuvenate" to describe the effect of alone time, and that's accurate. But it's more of a sluicing of layers we don't know are applied as we are constantly bombarded with societal messages. Many messages are subliminal and steer us away from our inner knowing. We begin to question our commitment to show up for ourselves and others with love and compassion. Alone time is necessary to shed the superficial and bring us back into alignment with our True Self.

Be cognizant of your alone time. Make sure it's filled with positive purpose, not crowded with self-pity. Be mindful of the push-pull process between self-care and self-sabotage. Every choice either lifts or lowers your energy. Some choices assist you while others work against you, and this may be hard to discern. Address your motives as honestly as possible to ensure a detrimental choice is not hiding under an ostensibly sound one. Is it healthful self-care or injurious isolation? Are you reconnecting with your soul or hiding from the world? Are you preparing for the rise or sinking further? Are you okay, or not? You know the difference.

If you want to be alone because you are in a bad mood, you're allowed to be. And you're allowed to be in a bad mood for the sole reason that you're in a bad mood. Irritability does not require validation, nor do you need to figure out every emotion. There doesn't need to be a reason behind the discontent; sometimes it just is. You are free to sit in an undiscoverable place while you wait for it to pass. There is a time to uncover the inner workings of your mind and heart, and there is a time to rest.

Remaining calm without answers to why you feel the way you do—another example of living in uncertainty—is a great expression of self-love and of trust. You love yourself enough to give yourself permission to simply exist when you need to, and you trust time to expose what's under your desire for solitude.

My marriage was saved because I allowed it to be saved. *We* allowed it to be saved. We were both all in (over time), and allowed the universe to provide people, professionals, and books that could offer solutions, and they came. Alignment with whom and what was available to us allowed the next steps to arrive. And the more we allowed, the more they showed up.

We allowed each other the room to grow on our own and as a couple. We took direction from Tracy and did what she told us to do, not perfectly and not as often as she suggested, but we tried. We learned a new language to dismantle arguments before they became bombs. We checked each other's temperatures to see how well we met the other's needs on the mental, emotional, spiritual, and physical fronts. We planned surprise date nights for each other and began to have fun again.

We did the work on ourselves and on us together. The healing around my family of origin transferred to our marriage. Forgiving my parents for their unhealed wounds and accepting our history as it's been—the triumphs and the mistakes—forced me to accept and forgive myself. My family lives inside me. They are a part of me, and I cannot resent them and expect to forgive myself, for we are one. Bridging an emotionally intimate, loving connection with my entire family tree, I am secure knowing I will always show up compassionately for myself. I'm safe to love Jim and let go of him should he die before me.

But forgiveness was not enough. Altering my perception was, and is, critical to how I show up in my marriage and for myself. Descending from my ancestors does not mean I am fated for their destiny. I'm free to change. When I notice behavior that mimics theirs, I evoke the power to choose a new thought pattern. That power translates to a boost in self-esteem, opening the door for new, healthy behaviors that increase my self-worth and self-love. A cycle of pain is replaced with a cycle of nourishment. It repeats, solidifies in my psyche and heart, and change occurs.

This inner work allowed me to invite Jim back into my heart space—into a new heart space because my heart had been through so much and had changed so much. My grief had spread its tentacles far into my core, twisting and turning it, even strangling it at times. When I untangled my grief after years of meditation and therapy, it was not the same heart that resided in my soul when Jim and I met. That's what life does. It changes us, and it mangles us, sometimes to the point of unrecognition. If we are brave enough to look deep into our hearts and souls and have the stamina to continue looking, we become recognizable once more, perhaps not with the same features but far better ones—ones that were always inside yearning to come forth.

Jim and I survived because we were brave enough to take a look at what was left after the untangling, at whom we became after life had its way with us. We walked each other through the intense emotions: the vulnerable discussions and the big, ugly tears of anger, frustration, sadness, and relief. We didn't stop crying until we were hugging. (I did most of the crying.) We dove into the deep, sacred space of shared intimacy, trusting when we surfaced we would be better for it personally, either together or apart. We happened to stay together. This is not everyone's story, nor should it be. What *is* everyone's story is the suffering, and the desire to run from it.

Don't run. Allow it. Feel it.

Let it wash over you until tears flow and you find yourself in a place where you feel closer to whole than you were before. Let yourself tremble as God swoops you up in the palm of His hand, wrapping you tight in His love and light, as if you are swaddled in the softest, snuggest blanket in the world, just as your first caretakers swaddled you before the love and light was shattered by their humanness.

Let your heart heal. Do not allow it to dissolve with painful loss. Do not bury your loving heart deep in a dark corner of past regret or future fear. Bring it out into the light and let your heart grow both softer and stronger during the trials. Allow it to endure through the joy and the pain no matter the events that may come to pass.

Allow yourself to be loved when you hurt. Then allow yourself to become love.

Then go love others.

EPILOGUE

Standing at the edge of the Atlantic Ocean, my mom rests in her beach chair fifty paces behind me. Her seasoned eyes gaze at the home of her beloved son's ashes as water laps at my ankles. Grandma Tessie's oldest grandchild and I, the youngest, soak our feet in the shallows. My cousin stares at the ocean, marveling at its clarity, as I eagerly anticipate the first Pearl Jam concert since Seattle. The show is on the evening of 9/11 in New York City. I muse about the uncanny date relevant to my marriage difficulties and reflect on all that has transpired the last four years—the pain and the growth. Anxiety hits, followed by calm.

Cupping saltwater in my hands, centuries of family dysfunction trickle through my fingers; eternal love seeps into my skin. A spontaneous letting-go-but-keeping ritual, I let Jeremy go to God as I welcome his essence into my heart; a part of him leaves while another part stays. My childhood trauma, shame, and self-sabotage float away in the sea foam. Heavy energy rolls out with the waves. Healing remains.

Inhaling deeply, smoothly, I am peacefully aware I'm doing my part. Carrying forth the healing work my ancestors began, I am forging a clearer path for my children to bring even greater peace to their souls, our family, and the world. It's the same path my parents bravely forged for me.

The lights go up on stage. Tears of relief fall from my eyes upon hearing the first lick of the guitar. I know the song instantly, and it could not be more perfect. Releasing the pain, I look up toward the heavens and thank my big brother for protecting me, still.

ACKNOWLEDGMENTS

Thank you to my biggest fan, the one who consistently offers the generosity of his beautiful spirit to me, Jim—a patient man who is loving and kind, who extends an immeasurable amount of grace to me even when I don't deserve it. Jim, your support and belief in me help me believe in myself. You bring out the best in me. You did all those years ago, and you still do today. I know you will continue to do so until your last breath.

Thanks to my daughters, who sacrificed precious time with me while I was hunkered down writing instead of watching Netflix, or when I jumped up from the dinner table and flew to my computer because I was struck with a thought I was afraid would escape me. When you are older and read this, please know every key stroke was for you: when you reach a chain, I hope you pick up this book and understand how to break it.

To my niece, Jeremy's daughter, may you always trust yourself and be all in, and may this book serve to show how powerful your dad is by gracing me with bravery to do this work. This power is in you too. *He* is in you.

To my New York therapist, Colleen Garvey, LCSW, and my Colorado therapist, Tracy Grant, MA, LMFT, you both have taught me much about the inner workings of my mind and my heart by shining the light on my darkness. You've called me out on the false stories I've told myself over the years and challenged me to face unpleasant facts about who I am and how I operate. Then you offered me a safe space to explore my shadow and the support to step into my truth. Tracy, thank you for taking the time to read parts of my first draft and for providing feedback regarding accuracy and flow, and for telling me to stop posturing!

Thanks to Jeffrey Berman, professor of a creative writing course I took at the State University of New York at Albany over twenty years ago. You taught me the most useful skill I can use as a writer and as a woman living with integrity. You said, "Show, don't tell." If I have learned anything in the four years I spent diligently professionalizing my drinking career in college it was to be a storyshower, not teller. I took that concept and applied it to my life: actions do speak louder than words. Thank you.

To Ms. Ganulin, my middle school music teacher who taught us to sing "The Rose" for our chorus performance in 1993, thank you for selecting this song. I had no idea how deeply it would resonate almost thirty years later. The lyrics to "The Rose" moved my feelings from the inside to the outside. And as my Carole says, "There's more room on the outside."

Shout out to the award-winning My Word Publishing crew: Polly Letofsky, I knew I liked you from the first curse word you dropped. You're my kinda gal: intuitive and real—no BSing with you. Thank you for using your keen insight to hook me up with an incredibly creative, smart, heartfelt, and hardworking team. To my editor, Bobby Haas, you encompass the perfect blend of spirit and intellect. Thank you for your constant support, your patience with my gazillion emails, and for your flattering commentary on my writing. You helped me believe in my talent as a writer. Then, you pushed me into the core of my vulnerability, to go places I didn't want to go in order to uncover the real story that was hiding underneath "fancy writing." You showed me how to deliver a "clear, concise, and compelling" message of pain and healing. This book would not be half of what it is without your guidance. Thank you Jan Stapleman, my fastidious proof editor with a sharp eye for not only grammar and punctuation but also for content issues, you professionally and respectfully pointed out a few concerns that did not cross my mind. Your edits made the messages more transparent. Kirsten Jensen, thank you for your knowledge, gentle suggestions, and practical guidance through every stage of this process. To Victoria Wolf, the most pristine graphic designer on the scene, you understood the concept from day one and created a beautiful cover portraying it masterfully.

Thank you to the super fantastic Sue McCormick for proofreading my first draft—for not only teaching me how to be a better writer by correcting grammar and sentence structure, but for calling me out on hypocritical and judgmental content. Thank you for holding my feet to the fire and for helping me keep the message pure. I need to send a thank-you card to Bill for bringing us together. To the boss, Carole Mueller, for reading (well listening to) parts of my first manuscript and giving me honest feedback, for reminding me, not just with your words but by your example, that kindness and compassion come first and to maintain those values from cover to cover, for your uplifting praise and your inspiring words. If the boss approves, you know you're on the right track.

To Rozi Cooper, who also read my first draft, for convincing me my story is relatable to so many people in so many ways, and that this healing message would be well-received. You gave me the courage and the will to dive as deep as I could with the hope other people would not only read, but feel, the words on these pages. Erika Montalbano, thank you for pushing me to self-publish. I am not sure this book would be presented to the world with as much Amanda in it if I did not go this route. And thanks for reading a chapter and pointing out my overuse of parentheses! Removing some of them made the message and the writing stronger. My voice became stronger. To my oldest *and* dearest friend, Linda Arcadipane, thank you for my initial website and, more meaningfully, for standing by my side through thick and thin, at the altar when Jim and I were married, next to me at Jeremy's funeral, and in a beach chair when I visit New York every summer. I know our love for one another and our commitment to friendship makes Poppy proud.

Thanks to my soul sisters: the women who helped me to recognize my authenticity by recognizing your own, who supported and encouraged me to walk boldly and unapologetically into mine. And thanks to the special women I have been blessed to know who were brave enough to share your vulnerability with me, providing me with a safe place to share mine. There are too many of you to list, but you know who you are.

Thanks to the men and women in various twelve-step recovery programs near and far who spoke much of the wisdom in this book. To those who walked alongside me on our journey toward emotional sobriety, you have given me an unparalleled education, one hour, one dollar (two now) at a time. I am indebted to you. Thanks to the actors who chose to meet me on the main stage of this incarnation, to love me, to hurt me, to heal me, and to teach me. Whether you've stayed or you've gone, I love you. You've made me the person I am today.

To you, the reader, who took a chance on me, not knowing exactly what you were getting yourself into but giving me your time and attention anyway, thank you. Special mention goes to my treadmill and my inspirational running playlist: without them I would not have experienced the lightning bolt moment when I knew I would and could write a book. I would not have been inspired enough to plunge into the dimensions of my soul with such fervor, nor would I have been able to make sense of my life experience with as much clarity if not for the music, lyrics, and endorphins.

My greatest thanks and utmost gratitude to the one with whom credit truly goes: my Higher Power, the Great Spirit Within, the intangible force for good that compels me to become a better version of myself with each breath I take, despite my occasional efforts to mess it up. Thank you for the intuitive messages and guidance you relentlessly impart. And for compelling me to open my mouth and share my/your voice with the world.

To my dad, thank you for your love of music and for introducing me to some of the greats at a young age. No matter how tough the road has been, I've had music to fall back on, to speak to me in ways I cannot speak to myself, to soothe me, and to inspire me to keep going. Our father-daughter relationship has had its challenges, and I'm grateful for the common ground we now meet on. I adore our connection and our friendship.

Last, but not least, my mother, Theresa: I have a huge amount of admiration and appreciation for you and your soul story. Thank you for showing me how to be resilient by being a true survivor, from cancer to divorce (both twice), to the loss of close friends and your entire family of origin, to the deepest cut of all—Jeremy's death. You often ask where I learned how to be the woman I am. From you. You show me how to love, to lose, and to do it again, and to rise from the pain with a servant's heart of dignity and love. I will always get back up because I've watched you do it.

To both of my parents for the lessons you've taught me through our mutual family experience: I would not have been pushed to the depths of healing if not for your mistakes and your successes, and most importantly, your love.

For that, I am grateful.

WORKS YOU MAY ENJOY

BOOKS

Walking Each Other Home by Ram Dass & Mirabai Bush

Warrior Goddess Training by HeatherAsh Amara

The Four Agreements by don Miguel Ruiz

Q&A The Buddha … Off the Record by Joan Duncan Oliver

The Ecstasy of Surrender by Judith Orloff, MD

The Universe Has Your Back by Gabrielle Bernstein

Braving the Wilderness by Brené Brown, PhD, MSW

You Are a Badass by Jen Sincero

The Power of Positive Thinking by Dr. Norman Vincent Peale

Living Buddha, Living Christ by Thich Nhat Hanh

Unlearn by Humble the Poet

O's Little Book of Calm and Comfort by The Editors of O, The Oprah Magazine.

The Dance of Anger by Harriet Lerner, PhD

You'll See it When You Believe It by Dr. Wayne Dyer

The Language of Letting Go by Melody Beattie

Many Lives, Many Masters by Brian L. Weiss, MD

POEMS & EXCERPTS

The Desiderata by Max Ehrmann

"Our Deepest Fear" by Marianne Williamson, from *A Return to Love*

"Sangha" by Danna Faulds, from *Go In and In*

ABOUT THE AUTHOR

A native New Yorker turned Coloradan, Amanda McKoy Flanagan blends street smarts with tree hugging for a pragmatic, yet soulful, approach to loving and losing; she is no stranger to either. Co-founder of the 501(c)(3) nonprofit organization, Castle Rock Clubhouse, a recovery clubhouse that serves as meeting space for various twelve-step programs, Amanda is passionate about sobriety, meditation, and spirituality. Through her commitment to climate action, she holds the spirit of loving-kindness, faithful perseverance, and compassionate service in high regard. A lover of horses, drumming, running, vegan eating, and dancing, she also enjoys singing with abandon to loud rock music.

Amanda holds a bachelor's degree from the State University of New York at Albany in English and journalism and a master's degree in social work from Stony Brook University, New York. Nevertheless, life has been her greatest teacher by far.

She lives in Castle Rock, Colorado, with her family and pup, Dolly.

Amanda is available for speaking engagements
and to join you for book club. Please contact her
at amanda@amandamckoyflanagan.com.

FB: www.facebook.com/amandamckoyflanagan

IG: @amandamckoyflanagan

TW: @amfauthor

Join the discussion at www.facebook.com/groups/allinbook

Visit amandamckoyflanagan.com for blog
posts and monthly newsletters.

ENDNOTES

1   Eddie Vedder, "Better Man," CD, track 11 on *Vitalogy*, Innocent Bystander (GMR) admin. by Universal Music Works (GMR), 1994. Used by permission. All rights reserved. International copyright secured.

2   Brené Brown, PhD, *Daring Greatly: How the Courage to Be Vulnerable Transforms the Way We Live, Love, Parent, and Lead* (New York: Gotham Books, 2012), 117-122.

3   Harville Hendrix, PhD, Helen Hunt LaKelly, PhD, *Getting the Love You Want: A Guide for Couples* (New York: St. Martin's Griffin, 2019), 7-8, 13, 25, 35.

4   Joe Vitale, Ihaleakala Hew Len, PhD, *Zero Limits: The Secret Hawaiian System for Wealth, Health, Peace, and More* (Hoboken, New Jersey: John Wiley & Sons, 2007), 139-142.

Made in the USA
Middletown, DE
05 November 2023

41991707R00139